Maureen Lipman was born in Hull when it was still Yorkshire and studied drama at LAMDA, where she received weekly food parcels from her bereft parents.

After three years with Olivier's Old Vic Company, she appeared in the West End in *Candida*, *Outside Edge*, *Messiah*, *See How They Run* and *Wonderful Town*, which won her the Olivier and Variety Club awards. Her one woman show *Re:Joyce* has had three successful seasons in the West End, in America and on BBC2 at Christmas time. In 1992 she appeared in *The Cabinet Minister* at the Albery Theatre, then opened at the Strand Theatre in Neil Simon's *Lost in Yonkers*.

Her TV series include *Agony*, *All at No. 20* (*TV Times* Award) and two series of *About Face* for Central Television. Favourite single plays are Jack Rosenthal's *The Evacuees* and *The Knowledge*, Alan Ayckbourn's *Absent Friends* and *Absurd Person Singular* and Richard Harris's *Outside Edge*.

Her films include *Up the Junction*, *Gumshoe*, *Educating Rita* and *Carry on Columbus*.

Her four books, *How Was It For You?*, *Something to Fall Back On*, *Thank You For Having Me* have all been on the bestseller lists.

D0860700

Also by Maureen Lipman:

HOW WAS IT FOR YOU?
SOMETHING TO FALL BACK ON
YOU GOT AN 'OLOGY?
THANK YOU FOR HAVING ME

When's It Coming Out?

MAUREEN LIPMAN

WARNER BOOKS

A *Warner* Book

First published in Great Britain in 1992 by Robson Books Ltd
This edition published in 1993 by Warner Books

Reprinted 1993

Copyright © 1992 Dramatic Licence Ltd

The moral right of the author has been asserted.

A CIP catalogue record for this book is
available from the British Library.

ISBN 0 7515 0602 8

Typeset in Plantin by Leaper & Gard Ltd, Bristol
Printed in England by Clays Ltd, St Ives plc

Warner Books
A Division of
Little, Brown and Company (UK) Limited
Brettenham House
Lancaster Place
London WC2E 7EN

For Rita Pearlman, my aunt.
A friend and confidante
when I was twelve,
an inspiration to me now.
With love.

Acknowledgements

Thanks to Louise Dixon, editor, who through constant exposure to my words has learned to shrug, gesticulate, pepper her prose with random 'chutzpahs' and 'schlepps' and still managed to make the kindest cuts of all.

Jacquie Granditer, my secretary, typing fast and flawlessly, and knowing what it says even when *I* can't read it.

Robson, J & C, for friendly persuasion and the ever-present promise of a French Egyptian meal and a contract.

Esperanza Maldanado, for keeping the home fires on simmer.

Dave the gardener, for the view from my rosewood desk.

Linda Kelsey, Sheena, Sue, *et al.* at *She* for deadlines and live coverage.

Sally Smith, for dressing me up and never letting me down.

For the lady at the signing session whose book I signed early on, and who then hung around the table, smiling and hovering, during a further half hour's signing, occasionally saying 'Well, I really should get going' or 'I'd best make a move then', but doing nothing about it.

'I don't think she's ever going to go,' I hissed to the publicity representative. 'There's something very odd about her.' At which point she came up yet again to make her 'Hello, I must be going' noises.

'OK then?' I said, heavily, 'nice to see you – got your book, have you? 'Bye then, see you again. 'Bye.'

She hovered some more, then said 'Yes, goodbye. It was lovely seeing you – must be going.'

'Yesss?' I intoned, even heavier.

'If you don't mind . . . could I have my pen back?'

And for Jack and the kids without whom there'd be no material.

And for Zelma without whom there'd be no me.

Contents

Prologue

Ladies and gentlemen, we are gathered here today for the grand opening of page one of this fourth volume of autobiographical badinage. Not bad going for someone who's, frankly, done little more with her life than keep her eyes open, her tongue alert and her Osmiroid filled.

Once again, we bring you the eclectic, egocentric, apoplectic and largely unconnected ramblings of a forty-six-year-old (or fifty-eight if you believe the birthday column of *The Times*) mother of two, wife of one, lover of . . . Radio Four, actress by character, author by accident, armchair socialist by inclination, telephobic by public demand, hot tempered, warm blooded, cold footed, idle, workaholic, sentimental, bullying, hypochondriac, health freakish, knock kneed, gnu-knecked, wasp waisted, fully paid up, clapped out member of the human rat race.

During the years you've been profligate enough to buy these angst ridden volumes, I've managed to collect one Olivier Award, one frozen shoulder, two astigmatisms, two Variety Club Awards, eleven telephones and one kiosk, a postbox, a wardrobe full of clothes I can never wear again because they've been on *Wogan* which dates me, several pat answers to the question 'How do you learn your lines?' and no answer at all to the question 'How do you get rid of your lines?', a gum shield, a caseful of forgotten good reviews and a heartful of remembered bad ones (i.e. 'a shocking waste of some of the finest mannerisms in the profession' *Jewish Chronicle*), floaters, fibroids, seventeen single earrings and twenty-four single socks and an unlisted phone number known by heart by every committee member in England and the Cinque Ports.

Due deference and reference will be paid to the man who removed me from the shelf just before my sell-by date was up. In those days, he sported a sports car, sideboards, a season ticket to Manchester United, a bachelor pad, a secretary, an office and a past.

Twenty years, three houses and fourteen sets of tumblers later, he's a man with distinguished temples, eleven telephones, two teenage offspring who regard him as a cute plaything, one mother-in-law who regards him as a concierge, one pair folding bifocals, one folding pipe, two folded musicals, several distinguished metal awards, a set of plastic cards and a plastic hip.

All that remains constant are his teeth, his temperament, his talent and, if you don't count that night in Valparaiso with Archduke Ferdinand of Hoëllegroton VI, his wife.

Shameless mention will be made of my children, Amy, eighteen, and Adam, sixteen, and my omnipresent mother, Zelma. Their lawyers have been alerted and probably bribed.

Are you absolutely sure this is what you had in mind when you said 'I fancy a nice read'? If so, put a drop of Windolene on your bifocals and turn over the page – you're a fool to yourself!

1

Household File

Leaving a Vacuum

'Which would you say is the dirtiest room in your house?' said the vacuum salesman to the actress.

'Do you mean in my opinion or in my mother's?' thought the actress grimly, but responded, instead, with 'Well, the kitchen – I expect.'

'Not so,' said Mohammed the salesman, for it was he. 'It is your bedroom. Are you aware that you shed your skin every four months and sweat one pint of liquid a night and all of that is in your bed?'

'As long as it's only in Jack's half,' quipped the actress.

It was a Saturday night and Jack and Adam and I were being entertained by this smart enterprising young man, in our own home, after a string of broken dates had caused me to slam the phone down on the Kirby Company saying, 'I don't care if it picks up more fluff than Rod Stewart, I wouldn't give your bloody vacuum houseroom.'

I say enterprising because pitching up on a Saturday evening with a smart suit and an 'I was just passing and I wondered . . .' smile is just the way to get straight into both my house and my room. We put the kettle on.

'Now what ever you think of it,' hissed my husband, caution being his middle name, 'don't buy it today, tell him you want to think it over.' I concurred in a smirking sort of way. I wasn't *going* to buy it. (I was going to *think* about it. For a year or so. Then I was going to entertain people with the story over dinner and then I was going to write it. To the accompaniment of Christine wielding the old wheezy Electrolux.)

I should explain the background to this unusual Saturday night beaver. Since, what I can only describe as our nuptials, some seventeen summers ago, we have hoovered our way through three residences and four vacuum cleaners. Each machine from Junior Hoover through Senior Hoovermatic to Elderly Turbo powered, increased in sleekness and two tone, multi-faceted plasticized glamour. Each machine, according to the weary engineer, majors in 'What we in the trade call "built in obsolescence"', a condition which applies to my son but not my latest Electrolux, which suffers more from premature ejaculation than early redundancy.

Christine (Tuesdays and Thursdays), who is what

my mother infuriatingly calls 'my woman', which makes me feel like a cross between Lady Bracknell and Vita Sackville-West, copes with the machine by alternately kicking it, and calling out in a hopeful manner 'Ja – a – a – ack! 'S'not workin' again.' Whereupon we call the engineer, the Christiaan Barnard of the vacuuming world, to transplant yet more new parts into this terminal three year old.

'They're not built to last you see,' chortles the engineer as we sign yet another docket. 'Cut your losses and get a new one – they're all the same.' By which he meant they're all lousy.

I vaguely shopped around – vaguely being the only way I know how to shop unless I'm in Joseph's of Knightsbridge. But, oh my! Cylinder or upright? Turbo or not Turbo? Miele or Bosch (could I sleep nights if I bought a German vacuum cleaner?) There are even machines which *tell* you when their bag needs changing. 'My bag is full' it whinges. I wondered if it would end up nagging me, like all the other speaking objects in my house, 'Shift your ass' it would snarl, 'just because you're on the telly, don't think you can push *me* around . . .'

So it was with some interest that I heard from my old friend Les (our friendly fireman who not only married our Swiss au pair, Ruth, but also gave Jack the inspiration for *London's Burning*), that he and Ruth had fallen in love with the Kirby cleaner, after an enlightening demo in their own home.

'I mean at *that* price,' laughed Les, 'I had *no* intention of *buying* it, NONE, but – I mean – this machine is unbelievable! It's . . . it's . . . it's phenomenal and they even take your old Hoover in part exchange!' For a moment I thought the normally prosaic Les was going to burst into song and levitate.

Instead, he told the tale of how the salesman had emptied a tin of salt on to the carpet, then swept it up thoroughly with their old Hoover, then put a clean bag into the machine and recovered another sackful of salt left behind by the previous vacuum.

'It sucks up to seven inches deep,' said the salesman.

'There's no answer to that,' said Les.

I booked a demo immediately, of course. Then, an hour before demo time, the firm phoned to say the salesman couldn't make it. Four days later I phoned them and made another appointment.

'Mohammed will call at eight o'clock. Thank you.'

At 8.45 Jack turned to me and said, 'Wasn't the vacuum cleaner salesman supposed to be . . .?'

The following day I phoned them and blew them out in a way I can only do at the end of a telephone, and told them where to stuff their upright . . . after all, if Mohammed won't come to Muswell Hill . . .

So you had to admire him for pitching up on the doorstep of a telephonic virago without an appointment, expecting a meat cleaver through his barnet.

'Oh my Lord, it's you!' gasped Mohammed (I hope I'm allowed to write that without having a death threat put on me!). 'It's The Telephone!

Beattie! Oh my heaven! Wait till I tell them at head office.'

So to the demonstration. Well, there is no question this gorgeous art-deco, aluminium robot can do everything your average 'woman' can do, and a few not even your lover can. Apart from shampooing, dry-cleaning, fluffing up, removing ceiling cobwebs, dusting, polishing and blow drying, it has attachments for spraying plants, sink plunging, sanding, blowing up *balloons*, massaging your HEAD and spraying sodding paint. I mean it just about stops short of making you a crème brûlée, but only just – and I reckon with the right attachment . . .

While Mohammed drew breath, I caught Jack's eye and launched into the old 'Well, it's very impressive, but my husband and I would like to think it over, it's an *awful* lot of money and . . .'

As I spoke, the old Hoover, in a fit of rivalry, vomited the contents of its stomach all over the patch it was supposed to be showing off on. Whereupon the husband in question – cautious Jack, remember? – interjected, in lordly fashion, to say, 'No, actually I think we should take it,' and produced the right kind of attachment for paying for it. Mohammed went home in prophet.

At the time of writing, Mohammed has been made Salesman of the Year and sent to Marbella as a bonus. We've never used anything but the vacuum head and the bed remains full of termites and sweat but it is a great investment and one day when Zelma gets off the Hull bus, tired and in need of succour,

I shall plug in the Kirby, get the balloons blown up and on the door and welcome her into my termite-free house with the offer of a shampoo and a head massage. What I won't do is tell her what it cost.

Whining and Dining

It was the Sunday before I had to leave for Plymouth, and we were going out for a Chinese meal. I was to spend three weeks by Plymouth Ho rehearsing a play, then to tour for six weeks before opening in the West End, and I was already feeling momentously guilty. The Sunday night dinner was in response to my daughter's winsome request for a 'real family, all together, last dinner'. This did a lot for the guilt.

The Chinese restaurant is a walk from our front door of no more than four minutes. By the time we reached its opaque, glass windows, Amy and I were locked in combative pose in identical states of prepubescent pugnacity, splitting hairs and infinitives.

How had it happened? Jack and Adam, sauntering behind us discussing 'Man's inhumanity to Man' and 'The Origins of Semantics', were agog to find us thus engaged. 'What's brought this on?' said Jack, knowing from past experience that worse was to follow. His son, equally adept at avoiding confrontation, glanced shiftily from side to side, fearsome of being overheard by the seaweed imbibing customers in the window.

Now, here's *my* side of it. I *think* I had made some casual/barbed remark, as in 'you will *help* Daddy while I'm away, won't you, darling – I mean table laying and the odd bit of help with the cooking?' Her nostrils and temper flared simultaneously, and the general pattern of her response centred around the *massive* amounts of domestic chores she did, compared with her totally indolent brother, every other girl at her school and every other person of her age in the entire civilized world and most of the Maldives. This coupled with sleep-deprivating amounts of A Level work which kept her hunched over her books till two in the morning was preposterous enough ... And now, apparently, I was demanding kitchen drudgery! Now, I could have laughed. I could have hugged her. I could have apologized and touched my forelock, or lightly remarked that I'd only wondered if it would be possible for her to peel her own avocado instead of my employing someone to come and do it for her. Instead I chose, characteristically, the path of most resistance.

Had *my* mother, the world's foremost authority on riot control procedures, only been with us, she would have poured meths on troubled waters by wailing, 'Aw, *don't* let's spoil everything. Come on, she didn't mean anything by it – did you lovey? We were all going to have such a nice *time*. Aahh, come-on! Everyone's looking! I've not been *well* – my heart's banging like a drum . . .' By which time, the family would have been seated in the restaurant, benignly shredding duck. Whereupon, mother would have remarked, 'all your Mam meant, Amy, was that your Dad is *ever* so tired and you don't really do much to help him – do you?' Then the whole thing would have started up again. For-tunately we never got that far. Instead we all went home, in silence, and I had to spend the rest of the evening cooking. It was not my evening for peaking – or Peking as it happened.

Neither my husband nor I can handle *rows*. We both grew up in exceptionally volatile homes and our idea of a good row tends to be, 'Oh right then, if that's what you think – thanks very much.'

'No, I didn't mean that.'

'Well. Neither did I . . . So there!'

Long pause. Then: 'Are you having a cup of tea?'

'Yeah. Do you want one or what?'

I mean, that's a really crucial explosion in our house. In fact, I have been known to *engineer* an argument just to clear the air. The trouble is, after it, I feel a hundred per cent better and Jack has to go to sleep for a couple of months to recover. Someone once said, 'If there are no arguments in a marriage, one partner is the underdog'. Oh God, I can almost hear him barking outside on the lawn.

All my best rows take place whilst driving in my

car. Alone. They are executed in a lucid, brilliant, barrister-like fashion which reduced my opponent to an amoeba. They tend to be between myself and anyone who's done me a real or imaginary wrong, and the full weight of my rhetoric is accompanied by tiny ironic changes of expression which I sometimes re-do in my driving mirror for added emphasis. This is all very satisfactory on the old A1 at forty miles an hour, but less so when faced with my foe in a two dimensional scenario, when the hyperbole becomes hysterical and the crystal-clear line of attack becomes defensive.

What's the definition of Italian Alzheimer's Disease? It's when you forget everything but a grudge.

Now I'm probably *less* Italian than Britt Ekland, but that joke rang a bell. I can have what's called in Yiddish, a 'broigus' with people who I don't even know. That's because I've walked out tight-lipped and conducted the row alone in my bathroom.

'I said I didn't want much taken off! You haven't cut my hair, you've revealed my scalp to the world! Look at me! I can't face going out! People stare at me as though I'm trying to audition for the *Crystal Maze!* What have you got against me? What have I ever done to you?' etc., etc.

Or:

'Why didn't you mention when I spent £80 on the trousers yesterday that the sale started today and that you'd be reducing them to £4.99? Well, fine. No, don't worry. I'll take my custom elsewhere – just because you're the only shop for miles which sells everything I *want* doesn't mean I need you.'

And why is it that when I do vent my spleen it's always the wrong time? Or the person I've vented it on has just had his mother kidnapped in a car boot or lost his house in a freak landslide or developed myxomatosis? And within seconds of my outburst I'm back where I was before I began it. In the wrong.

Why do women have such problems expressing their anger? The answer is as clear as the view from my Plymouth hotel window. It's not ladylike, is it, old girl?

Oxford Blues

My eighteen year old daughter is a self-confessed dumb brunette. She specializes in the kind of high drama which makes *Total Recall* look like *Milly, Molly, Mandy*. Her idea of a long walk is from the front door to the car door, and her idea of a safe place in which to keep her money is in her friend Melanie's jacket pocket. Only last night, she left me a note which read, 'The cat is incontinent. She did a pooh on my Chaucer. We'll discuss it tomorrow. Yours, Monkfish.' (She also seems to have inherited her grandmother's somewhat prurient attitude to sex, best summed up in the word 'Urrghh!')

It was with some trepidation, therefore, that I took Amy to Victoria Station recently, to undertake a lone journey, of ten stops, to visit Melanie's music course in Bickley. I had curled the odd lip when told of this proposed expedition, and even ventured a sarcastic, 'But won't you be worried on your own-ikins on big iron horse in countryside, darling?'

'No, I won't,' she replied. 'I've got Gabriel Garcia Marquez, and Melanie's meeting me. All I do is count the stations, stand up at station nine and get off at station ten.'

We travelled, by car, to Covent Garden, where I had a wig fitting, then I guided her towards the tube station: she looked aghast: 'Aren't we going to Victoria by cab?'

'No, we're not. It's only a couple of stops.'

'But . . .'

'No buts. It's good for you.'

'I don't mind – it's you I was thinking about. You'll get stared at and people will complain to you about their phone bills and you won't like it.'

'I'll love it,' I muttered grimly as I grappled with the baffling technology of the ticket machines. (Times have certainly changed since it was all done via a queue and a surly attendant behind a mucky glass panel.) A mere six or seven minutes later I'd found the right money and the machine (no less surly than its predecessor) had spat out my tickets on to the tessellated tiles. I was pleased as punch. Amy was a tense presence at my side, her eyes darting from left to right for fear of incipient muggers. Some muggers do 'ave 'em, I thought to myself.

As we surged into the lift two bells rang sharply and Amy jumped three feet in the air like a cartoon rabbit, rolling both eyes independently of one another.

'What's that?' she hissed, digging ten nails deep into her mother's pre-stressed linen jacket.

'Two bells ringing, dear,' I replied. 'To tell you the doors are closing.'

She relaxed her grip and my arm went back to its normal colour.

As we walked down the corridors, a group of large teenage boys began to run through, past and around us on their way to the train. The noise was deafening, but they were harmless enough. My companion thought otherwise, however, and flattened herself against the wall in a fair impersonation of Jeff Goldblum in *The Fly*, until the last one had passed.

'Darling,' I remonstrated, 'you really must *relax*. *Nothing* is going to happen – just look the other way and they'll pass you by.'

We arrived early at Victoria. I was all for a coffee and a prune Danish but no, apparently we had to find out what platform the train left from. The Information Bureau must be sought. Was sought. Was closed. BR weren't bothering with information that day. Well, it was Friday – people would have the whole weekend to get back to where they should have got to if they'd had the information. A weary guard stood by the Sock Shop, fielding enquiries like Paddy Ashdown on *Any Questions*. He flinched only slightly on my approach.

'Why is the Information Bureau closed?'

'We're understaffed.'

'Obviously. Well, can you tell me what platform the train to Bickley leaves from?'

'Platform three.'

'Thank you. Can you tell me something else?' he looked wary, as well he might. 'Why don't they put *you* in the Information Booth?'

'Because I'm not Information.'

'Oh. Sorry. My mistake. Thanks for the Information.'

I got her on to the train. It seemed fairly empty.

'Will you wait till it goes?' she asked querulously – honestly it was like shepherding Countess Alice of Athlone around, not a spry young teenager.

'Yes, darling,' I gritted. 'But honestly, nothing will happen – you'll be fine.' I stood grinning inanely for ten minutes, until the train took her pinched little face from sight.

'I've over-protected that child,' I chuntered as I walked back towards a sign which read something ominously like 'Any person leaving without a ticket is subject to a fine of nine million Ecus or a lifetime in Reading gaol.' (I attempted to explain to the far from kindly ticket collector that I was not a fare dodger from Felixstowe, but the mother of an over anxious teenager from Muswell Hill.)

When I arrived home Mr Rosenthal's face was indigo. His mood blue.

'She rang,' he grumbled, 'from Bickley station.'

'Why? What happened?'

'Nothing happened. She rang because she'd found the kitchen phone in her handbag. She was bringing it downstairs and she forgot to put it back. That child has no common sense whatsoever.'

I must say, for once, I didn't share his anger. I hooted with laughter. This apple was certainly not falling far from the tree.

It was only on her return that we learned the true nature of the journey.

'Oh, by the way,' she said calmly after demolishing one and a half dinners. 'The man who sat opposite me on the train had no front to his trousers.'

The silence was the first of its kind in our kitchen for sixteen years.

'What do you mean no front to his trousers?' asked my mother, from whom Amy has also inherited a good deal of her fear of the unknown.

'Well. He just had a huge hole where the front of his trousers should have been. It was revolting.'

'But – I mean – did – was he? Could you . . .? What did you do . . .?'

The family was agog.

'Oh nothing. I just looked quickly from one window to the other, like an umpire. I caught a glimpse of pink but I couldn't be *altogether* sure whether it really was his thingy or if he just had a bag of marshmallows and a sausage in his lap.'

It took a while to restore any semblance of order to the dinner table. One or other of us kept dissolving into our desserts until finally my mother cracked it, as only my mother can, by saying, 'Are you sure it wasn't just a little tear in the front of his trousers? It could happen to anyone.'

'Grandma. His trousers were completely open. There was no front. They were *late* trousers – those trousers had ceased to be. They . . .'

'He actually had "flasher's" trousers on, Mum,' I explained.

She was horror-stricken – but, predictably, not for the reason you'd expect.

Don't tell me you can *buy* them in London?'

Once the A level year begins, though, there is little time for travel, or fun. Or merriment of any kind. Just pure sweat, long days in stuffy rooms, tetchiness and panic. Things are tough for the A level student. They are also tough for the A level student's parents and the state of the A level student's bedroom, temper, family doctor and ageing cat. It's the way it creeps up on you. For a few months in the summer vacation you tend to say gingerly to your flame-tempered progeny, 'Have you got your UCCA forms sorted out?' Only to hear:

'No. Nobody has. Nobody does it till we get back. There's *ages*, don't go *on* about it, nobody else's mother ever mentions it. Honestly!'

So you shut up until she's the only one whose form hasn't been completed and it's your fault for taking her on a holiday in France to speak the subject instead of leaving her at home to register for it.

Then the form gets filled in for the wrong year and the words 'We told you to do it in pencil' wither and die on your lips as the Tipp-Ex makes its guest appearance from under the living room sofa where the cat last pushed it. The dried-out Tipp-Ex. (No, honesly, the white lumps look good on the rust upholstery, really, they do.)

Then the choices of University seem to be made by such infallible yardsticks as 'Have you seen the ratio of men students to female?' or 'It's so pretty in the brochure – there are roses round the door.' And UCCA forms, thicker and whiter in some places than others, go off.

Then three months before the mock A Levels, gaga parents are informed, casually over lamb chops, that she will sit for the Oxford exam first. How to handle this? Pride bursting out through your polo neck you say, '*You* darling? Are they sure?' and receive pretty much what you deserve. So the whole family, including the mother's mother, pile on to the M4 in search of it. Tip number one. When viewing Oxford, park in the first car park you see marked 'Car Park'. Even if it's in Leatherhead – otherwise you too can spend several moist hours in the car, crawling at a sloth's pace around a one-way system developed by the same person who was responsible for any large NHS hospital, the Pompidou Centre and probably the human intestine.

Then come the two exams. The first is three hours long and she sets off for it as thin, tapering and white as a Friday night candle. The amount of work done in the weeks before was Herculean. Every night as we went to bed her midnight oil was recycled and used again. My dining room became the New

British Library and took as long to clear up as the original has to build.

And afterwards? Disaster! Hopeless! Answered all the wrong questions, wrote gibberish, now they'll just think she's a madwoman and she won't even *get* an interview which is fine 'cos she never wanted to go there until they told her she had to. By now my seventeen year old and seven of her friends are whey-faced skin and bone. She's lost eight pounds but that's nothing compared to Marina who's lost a stone and Pikka who went dizzy on a radiator.

Now we wait for three weeks (or three years depending on your point of view or your postman) to see if she is 'de-summoned'. This heinous practice involves an Oxford interview date given two to three weeks ahead. However, at any time during that period, the college can ring the school with a rejection based on the exam result. This leads to retrospectively hilarious scenes where a perfectly serene girl doing an experiment in the lab can see the approach of a beckoning headteacher wearing a sympathetic wince, and choose between accompanying her outside to hear her fate or setting fire to herself with a Bunsen burner.

The day before the projected interview, the girl with whom Amy was to travel was de-summoned. Apparently one poor child – for children they are and you wouldn't actually treat a fruitbat this way – made it as far as the railway station, where she was de-summoned by a message on the electronic information board. Now *there's* thoughtful.

The day before the Tuesday interview, Amy set
out alone for Paddington like a piece of condemned
Spam. We daren't risk her travelling on the morning
of the interview because of BR's tendency to halt the
train because the driver has seen a moth on the
tracks. For two and a half days the phone brought
us, 'It's freezing here, I've got one blanket and
Marina's only got a sheet and . . .'

'Yes but how did the interview g–?' Beep-beep-
beep . . .

'It's character building,' I told her distressed
father. For *him* I meant.

At two-thirty on Wednesday, she left Oxford with
the vague idea that if she hadn't heard within a
further three weeks she could ring the college to find
out. This system has been thought out by very clever
people. But then so was the Chinese Water Torture.

Over the next few weeks the drop-out rate was one
every two days. Rejection I mean. And when the
surefire candidate, a bright brilliant, ten GCSEs at
grade 'A' girl was rejected we stopped caring. Who
the hell wants to learn Anglo Saxon in an almshouse
anyway? 'Leofsunu Gemaelde ond his linde ahof to
gebeorge he tham beorne oncwaeth.' What's that
got to do with the price of lentils?

The Saturday morning letter was almost a relief.
Jack was up at eight staring at the envelope. Adam
and I held it under the kitchen light until ten-thirty
deciphering nothing but the words 'inform you' and
when, at eleven, the exhausted candidate wandered
blearily in, she puts us out of our misery with a

rueful grin, and a request for a hearty breakfast.

So now what? Eight out of eight girls rejected. Then they must write grovelly letters to all the universities who wouldn't consider their applications until Oxford was resolved and shift their thin weary limbs into second gear to start the *real* business of *mock* A levels. What an excellent introduction to life's early redundancies.

I can't help wondering if Oxford University's definition of 'one-way system' is the same as the *Oxford Dictionary*'s.

August. It's all over now, bar the shouting, and the girl did herself proud. And us! The exams, their aftermath and the waiting for results were a torment, but it was worth it. Almost the loveliest part was when we heard that Lizzy's daughter, Sarah, born on the same day as Amy, had got precisely the same A B B grades.

Can you *do* a degree in astrology, they wonder?

Sofa so Good

It was a bleak and wintry Thursday when the family chesterfield died. This wasn't entirely unexpected, it had been sickening for some time. (Even so, the suddenness of her demise – not entirely unconnected with my son's congenital need to fling himself horizontally on to it from a distance of eight feet two or three times an hour – was a shock.)

First the castors shot off in a westerly direction, closely followed by two legs, east and north, north-west. Then the seating cushions spontaneously imploded revealing toys we haven't seen since *Star Wars*, the arms inverted into a sort of shrug, she gave a long, deep sigh and her back buttons popped off. It was clear that this was, at best, a late chesterfield, soon to be despatched to the Great Furniture Repository in the Sky.

The problem is that this was one irreplaceable

sofa. It was more than just an obscure object of design. It was ... well, it was almost part of the furniture. It came with Jack. It was virtually his dowry. It was accompanied by some paintings, a desk, two grey jerseys and a complete set of Peter Sarstedt LPs.

When we moved down South into rented accommodation, it lived patiently in 'kennels' in Blackpool until we became first-time home-owners. (This, you understand, was in the days when 'the chain' was something you locked up your bike with and a recession was the space on either side of your mantelpiece.) In time we sent for the chesterfield and she took her rightful place on the ginger twistpile – our 'Lasting, Casting Couch'.

Over the next seventeen years, out-of-work actresses 'rested' on it, confirmed bachelors 'camped' on it, a baby daughter pee-ed down and a baby son pee-ed up on it and the family feline, practising her famed impersonation of a shredding machine all around it, gave it the look of one of PJ Proby's discarded waistcoats.

The whole thing came to a head on the night of our 'Come as You Were' party, when I saw Denis Norden, six foot three, and Lesley Joseph, five foot one, at each end of the settee. Lesley was considerably taller than Dennis. The sofa, like most of my guests, was legless.

'The Sales are on,' said Mother, the Humberside Oracle. 'Come on, we'll go to John Lewis and you can change that lampshade you've had cluttering up the floor all these months, and then we can do Selfridges, they're bound to have what you want. What *do* you want, actually? A three-seater or two two-seaters? Armchairs are nice, mind you. Have you thought about re-upholstery? There's nothing wrong with that couch really and whatever you get that cat will make "ashenblotty" out of it.'

By the time we reached John Lewis my brain was on circuit jammed. Rain was pouring down in biblical fashion and I parked on Level three. There was no lift. Words were exchanged. We made it through the deluge and legged it to Lewis's.

'Look at the price of those chandeliers,' said Mother shaking out her rainhood on to a Donald Duck desk-lamp. '£150. That's what my parents, God rest their souls, paid for their first house.'

I stood in the queue with my lampshade.

'Why are you standing in the queue?' she demanded. 'Why don't you speak to the man walking around? Your Uncle Issy always said, "go to the man at the top".'

'There is no man at the . . .'

'Excuse me. Are you there? My daughter bought this lampshade . . .'

I'm dying. Water is dripping down parts of me that only my acupuncturist knew I had, my skirt is suctioned to my thighs and I'm suffering from terminal embarrassment. The queue has begun to titter. Mrs Jones lives.

She's right, of course. We make the exchange and, leaving the new shade for a later pick-up, we head for the furniture department which instantly yields a rose-pink chesterfield at a 'Have we gone raving mad?' reduction. Mother is horrified and says to a passing assistant, 'Excuse me. Are you there? Would you say this was a serviceable fabric for a family with two teenage children and a cat, I mean? Has it been Scotchguarded? There you are – you'd be *much* better off with a patterned Dralon.' It was time to be blown to Selfridges.

'My coat's drenched through,' grumbled Mum. It was my fault and I knew it. 'I'll have a job to dry it before I catch that bus back to Hull tomorrow.'

I put my foot down. (Always a mistake when you're standing in six inches of rain.) 'Come on,' I said, 'we're going home. I can get a couch any time.'

Mother stood stock-still as if she'd been freeze-framed. 'Home?' She gave the word three syllables and several changes of key. '*Go home?*' You'd think I'd suggested a stop off at a Pork Scratchings Shop. 'Whatever for? We're only five minutes from Selfridges. You'll be sorry. You'll kick yourself.' Little did she know as she squelched heroically on her way that I already was.

Finally we slid into the dry warmth of the Handbag and Hosiery Department and thence into Furniture. '*You* look,' moaned Mother as she sank into the first available sofa-bed, 'I've had it.'

I looked. I saw. I sat upon. It was perfect. An Elizabethan-style sofa with brass knobs on. Literally. One small point. It was upholstered in ivory silk moire. How was I to hide that fact from . . .

'Have you gone mad!' came a voice I knew and often loved. Too late. I'm nabbed. 'You're not thinking of cream, Maureen ... Excuse me, Miss, are you there? What we need is something to go on a green carpet, have you got such a thing?' Given such a wide brief, the saleslady could only think of one thing to say...

'Well, if it's good enough for Mrs Jones, it's good enough for ...'

Mother caught up with me somewhere in Oxford Street and we grimly monsooned our way back to the car park.

'You get the car, I'll pick up the lampshade,' she said, undaunted by the John Lewis security man locking the last customer out of the store. As I dashed across the square to the car park, I heard, 'Excuse me. You've got to let me in. I'm catching a train to Hull in half and hour and if I don't have that parcel with me I shall lose my job and everything.' He let her in.

'Closed. Please use entrance on other side of Square', said the NCP entrance. I paddled back, cursing pleasantly and finally climbed back into the car, pausing only to lower the brim of my trilby and release a pint and a half of acid rain on to the driver's seat.

Much later, as we sat sniffling in our bath-robes, the chesterfield and the delinquent tabby seemed to be regarding us with mutual smugness: 'Need a psychiatrist, those two,' they seemed to be saying, 'not a ruddy couch!'

*

It's eighteen months since I went out looking for that sofa. We still don't have a new one. The chair and the existing sofa's been minced into a sort of chilli con carne by the delinquent cat and I've taken to throwing throwovers, American style, over them, which fools no one. Decorating time has rolled round again but I think it would be simpler all round just to move. The kids go apoplectic at the thought, but they'll be off and gone soon. Living in rodent infested student digs with ovens which open of their own volition on account of the livestock left in them. And Jack and I have had Muswell Hill. The journey in and out each evening to the theatre drives me to distraction, particularly since 'The Jamesons', the radio equivalent of chalk on a blackboard or finger-nails on a frying pan came into being. We're ready for Maida Vale or Belsize Park, if the lottery comes up. I mean what are we doing here in the first place anyway?

Well. It is of course, a well documented fact that when we northerners head south to do our chosen thingy in't capital, we invariably settle in the north-ern sector of town. This is a double-edged sword as it placates our guilt, marginally, at forsaking our roots and it re-roots us near enough to the M1, that should the going get tough in Tufnell Park, then the tough can speedily get going.

As a student in the mid-Sixties, I was puzzled to find myself the only resident of Earls Court who didn't hail from Alice Springs, and a brief flirtation

with Battersea was merely an actorish homage to my
landing a plum role in the film of *Up the Junction*.

Time, opportunities and the mating cry of the
unwed twenty-five-year-old drew me to Manchester
where I met the man who was to become my
co-mortgagee. When we both returned to 'The
Smoke', it seemed only right and proper to settle in
leafy Hampstead, after such a protracted stay in Fog
Lane, Didsbury.

In retrospect, I think Jack was more in love with
Hampstead than he was with me – well, to be fair, he
saw more *of* it. I worked at the Old Vic in Waterloo
understudying and playing in a repertory of six
different plays and, honest 'native of North America', I cycled to and from Waterloo leaving at nine in
the morning and returning at 11.45 at night, carrying six scripts and an expanding seven foot square
crocheted blanket in my front basket. I arrived home
on all fours, scarlet faced and incapable of speech. I
was very happy.

More time, more mating calls and the patter of
tiny accountants, deemed the Rosenthals in need of
a house and, being a cautious bent, that meant
moving further out. Or *in* if you allow for the fact
that we were still, basically two northerners.

Thus, we found ourselves in Muswell Hill. We
found our dream house nesting in the skirts of
Alexandra Palace and, in the shadow of that beige
elephant, our children learned to ride bikes, row
boats, throw sand at smaller children and make
cynical remarks about the One O'Clock Club.

In floods of tears we watched from our terraced garden as the grand old lady burned down and died, and in a spirit of Victorian jubilation we watched her rise like a dodo from the dust. Many and oft are the Sundays we've wandered aimlessly round antique shows, budgie shows and exhibitions of macramé pinafore dresses and peanut flavoured meatballs by women from obscure Caribbean islands, had a paper cup of re-cycled tea and watched *homo sapiens* rediscover his ability to rest on four legs on the dry-ski slope.

Nowadays the kids take picnics there with their friends and refuse to visit the brand new ice-skating rink on the grounds that they'd rather stay home with *Thelma and Louise*. Personally I've never understood how anybody ever *gets* there – no tube. But get there they do – in their thousands. The garden centre and its tea room make *Joseph and the Amazing Technicolor Dreamcoat* look like this season's flop, though personally I've yet to go there when they're not stacking up the chairs, striking the Eccles cakes and whistling 'The Party's Over'.

We're also just within frisbee-ing distance of glorious Kenwood – a great place for taking visiting Americans as you can kill the stately home and the parklands of London lust in one fell swoop. Highgate cemetery will impress your Baltic penfriends less than it was wont to, and Crouch End is just near enough to us and to town, to hold a media lunch date.

Of course the greatest act of gazumping came with

the addition to the area of Marks & Spencer PLC. It turned us instantly from 'Up and Coming' into 'Fashionable and Desirable'. The fact that it's only a food hall and you still have to travel three miles for a pair of pyjamas is by the by. Or a tea towel. Or a sheet. Or a decent pair of shoes.

Still, pouring in, they come. Give me your student nurse, your struggling thespian, your batty conservationist, your first-time floor sander, your afternoon telly presenter, your Cypriot wholesalers, your Muswell Hill yuppies – Muppies if you like – all human life is here. But only if they have a bus pass. Still no tube line, Wheelie-Bins, Leisure Centre, decent library or swimming pool. And for some unaccountable reason the highest poll tax in England.

So, why am I still here? Erm . . . basically because I like the house and I'm passionate about the garden – I'd have to take it with me. No, really. Some people take light bulbs and fireplaces and fitted shelves and brass doorknobs. Not me. I'd be carrying five tons of earth, two wistarias, one stone urn, one pillar box, fourteen flowering yuccas, three bleeding heart bushes, two chimney pots filled with magenta petunias, some flaming pyranus, a mass of Canterbury bells and a thriving passion flower. And that would be my *first* load. I'm also as indolent as a basking cat, there's an excellent cheese shop, I like the view and tea chests give me hives.

Raising Arizona

A SHORT SCREENPLAY

EXTERIOR: Street. Hot day in Muswell Hill. A woman is carefully carrying a plastic bag. She is within twenty yards of her home when footsteps behind her accelerate and a hand touches her arm.

He: 'Excuse me. Sorry to bother y . . .'
She: 'Aaaargh! Christ, you frightened me – don't *do* that!'
He: 'Sorry, sorry, it's just that, I mean, I know who you are . . .'
She: 'Oh, jolly good. So do I, but you really mustn't go touching strange women just because you know who they are.'
He: 'I know. I'm sorry. I . . . Oh God. The thing is,

I mean, er – have you got a minute? Can I talk to you?'

He is twenty-five but looks nineteen. Thin, dark, unshaven chin, puppy dog eyes, longish floppy brown hair. The chest hairs which bedraggle out from his sleeveless vest belie his tender years and the brown leather jerkin spell street cred rather than student unrest.

She: (placing the plastic bag on a low wall.) 'It's a cheese dish. Old. It's a present from my daughter to her English teacher, what did you want to say to me?'

He shifts his weight. She smiles because he really is ducking and weaving like someone in an early Montgomery Clift movie. She wants to help but not quite as much as she wants to get home and remove whatever it is that is pressing her little toe into a throbbing pulp.

She: 'Are you an actor?'
He: (Astonished) 'No.'

There is a 'why' in his response. He doesn't realize that eighty per cent of the people who stop her in public places do so because: a) They have a niece who knocks spots off Barbra Streisand and can't get an Equity Card; b) They have just won the Beerbohm Tree Award at the Basingstoke Academy of

Performing Arts and they just need a few thousand to see them through the next term; c) They think she was mad to give up those commercials, they haven't seen much of her on TV since, and hasn't she gone thin?

He: 'No, I'm not working at the moment – well, I mean I'm in Sainsbury's Homebase just to make, you know, to live, but the thing is, I know it's ridiculous and why should you be remotely interested – but look. My theory is, that if you don't go for it when you've got the chance then . . .'
She: 'Go on. What's the problem?'

She slips off one shoe and massages the toe tortuously against her other foot.

He: 'Well. The thing is . . .'

His face changes as into shot comes a young girl. She is shorter and sturdier than he, cropped blonde hair, adolescent skin, gamine features and she is looking at him underneath her lashes as a mother would look at a kid who's asked a strange lady why bits of her wobble like that, is it 'cos she's so fat?

He: 'This is Robin. This is the woman I love.' (The woman he loves shakes her head in despair). 'She has to go back to America on Sunday. Thing is I can't live without her. She's . . . I don't have the money to go back with her. So I thought . . . well . . . what can you lose? That's . . . it.'

Pause.

She: 'You are asking me to give you money so you can follow your girlfriend to America?'

He: 'I just saw you. I'm desperate. Like I said if you don't go for it in life . . .'

She: 'Yeah, yeah – but what are you going to do when you get there? You can't work there. You won't get a permit, unless you get married.'

He: 'We're going to get married. That's the idea. That's it. We can't exist without one another – it's the rightest thing that's ever happ . . .'

She: 'Look, you do understand, I can't just, I mean I'm constantly being asked . . .'

He: 'I *know*.'

She: '. . . for money.'

He: 'Look, I've a letter from her parents saying how much they like me, if that would do any good.'

She: 'How much do you need? A one-way ticket to New York – £179 on Virgin, isn't it?'

He: 'Well, no – you see it's Arizona so it's £409, and you have to get a return or they don't let you . . .'

She: '£409! Hold on, hold on – look. Wait.' (She turns to the girl, Robin, whose head is down). 'What are you going to do with him when you get him to Arizona?'

Pause. Robin raises her eyes. Shakes her head again and in a scarcely audible whisper says:

Robin: 'Oh, I don't know . . . Jes love him.'

For reasons best known to a Freudian she once visited, uncontrollable tears stream down the cheeks of the total stranger. She walks around in a circle on her good foot and takes pot shots at herself but gravity is inexorable and they trickle beneath her sunglasses. She struggles with her wobbling thorax.

She: 'What's needed here is a second opinion. From a rational person. I'm hopeless. Quick. Give me your name and address, I need to think . . . here . . .'

She replaces the sandal and gives him first her cheque book, then and for fear of giving the wrong impression, a cleaning ticket to write on. Goodbyes are tentative and she finds herself kissing them and wishing them happiness. She limps home blearily, rings the doorbell. A middle-aged man wearing hornrimmed glasses and two warring fabrics opens the door. His face changes from welcoming to concerned in a millisecond.

Husband: 'Hello lu . . . what's happened? Tell me. What's the matter?'

He takes the cheese dish and sits her down. She's

still weeping but now with the odd gurgle of laughter because she knows his concern will be temporary. It is. Throughout her dramatized reconstruction we linger on his face, as it turns into the kid and the fat lady expression.

He: 'You're bloody mad,' he says, not unkindly.
She: 'But I should have just given him the money. They were so – beautiful. I mean, it could have been Romeo and Juliet!'
He: 'Or Bonnie and Clyde.'
She: (Sighs) 'Yeah, well.'

Enter her daughter, eighteen, whey-faced and A--levelled, and her son, fifteen, who has recently learned to whistle tunelessly. They've heard the bare bones of the story from LSF (as in long-suffering father) and want confirmation from the HM (as in horse's mouth).

Daughter: 'But who *were* they? Had you met them before? I mean what did they say to upset you and did you give them any-thing?'

The camera stays on the children's faces as their mother ruefully explains.

She: 'It's just that they were so young. And so passionate. I don't know, I just feel as if I should have given them a chance.'

Daughter: 'You should have. Changing someone's
          life. It's so romantic. Can't you run after
          them?'
Son: (Glancing up from sponge ball attached to his
          sock) '*I* think you should have told them to
          bugger off.'

THE END

The woman with the cheese dish has since a) lost the
cleaning ticket; b) worked out that her royalties
would easily take the young man to Arizona and c)
awaits his call.

Pie Chart

A plum tree has arrived in my back garden. Complete with plums. Scores of them. Plump, juicy, purple and, I'm told, edible. The thing is that I'm convinced it's a miracle, or osmosis, or somebody else's tree. It's also standing in the spot where the apricot tree used to be. The one which was struck by lightning so that all the apricots shrivelled into little beige scrotums.

Still, there is it, large as life and twice as fruitful. I only noticed it as I was picking up cooking apples from the lawn.

'I must pick those apples up from the lawn,' I remarked hopefully to the family. 'They'll go all brown if I don't.' The family continued staring at their typewriters and their Test Match, so sometime later I retrieved the said apples. Six green firm ones and twenty-seven brown sodden ones. I shook the branches vehemently, but the apples clung on for dear life until the moment I departed, apple-laden, for the kitchen, whereupon they flung themselves, kamikaze fashion, to the floor shouting 'Take me, I'm yours' to the waiting vermin. No wonder they make such good *tarts*.

'Come on Amy,' I heard a woman's voice say. 'Let's make some fruit pies.' Amy and I looked round in unison to see who'd uttered such an ominous sentence in this our very own and Small-boned kitchen, but there were only the two of us there. The woman's voice continued: 'You peel the apples and I'll stew the plums.' It was becoming obvious by the pop-eyed look on my daughter's face that the insane voice belonged to her mother.

I propped up the short pastry recipe against the microwave six or seven times before tearing it out and taping it to the wall. I found the kitchen scales and carried the only bag of flour we had to the work surface. It was rye flour.

'It'll be fine,' my daughter informed me. 'Flour is flour.' This was our second big mistake. The first was picking up the apples.

By now the plums were stewed. Well and truly. Two pound of plums had reduced without skin and stones to a couple of tablespoons of warm purée. We decided, of necessity, that we would use this to flavour the apples, and I got down to some serious mixing and kneading. I'd seen my mother do it often enough over the years. 'Would Jack like a nice meat and potato pie?' she'd ask rhetorically. Would he?

Second only to seeing Bobby Charlton knighted he'd like a meat and potato pie.

'S'alright,' I comforted myself, 'he didn't marry me for my ruff puff, anymore than I married him for the shine on his choux.'

The dough, for want of a more accurate word, was a collector's item. Grey in hue, it had the consistency of reject clay and a wonderful sense of humour. By that I mean it broke up every time I came near it. And it took to the rolling pin in the same way as Andy Capp does to Florrie's after a long and robust evening in 'The Stoat and Firkin'. After an hour of flouring the board, the work surface, the floor, the telephone and the cook, I was drained. My legs hurt from standing, my wrists hurt from rolling and my daughter's ears hurt from the sound of her mother cursing flour in general, and wholemeal rye flour with natural fibre added, in particular.

'Just lay it down in strips, Mod,' she beseeched. 'I can stick the bits together with water.' Grudgingly I complied, peeling two and a half inch clumps off the rolling pin and passing them over to the master pastry cook across the table. Patchwork Pie – a cottage industry sprang up before our eyes.

In minutes we'd covered the pie dish, in seconds we added the apples and in triumph we laid the remaining strips over the fruit and hurled the whole thing unceremoniously into an oven which had been pre-heating for almost two hours.

I'd like to report that all was well in the end and that a new chapter had ensued in this heretofore 'pastry-free zone' – but you'd know by my face that I was lying. When we removed the travesty from the oven some fifteen minutes later, it was crispy to a fault, severely undercooked and abhorrent to the nose. At one and the same time.

We tried, God knows, we tried. Jack had a brave mouthful, said 'Mmmmmm' as in 'Ah Bisto' and headed for the wastebin in a manner which could best be described as clandestine. The two cooks noisily left their plates almost as full when they'd finished as when they'd started. Which just left Adam, innocently watching the Old Trafford test match, from a prone position on the living room floor. A lot of giggling ensued as we poured an unusually generous portion of cream over an enormous slice of pie.

Some time later we went in to collect the dish.

'How was it?' I asked, all innocence and candour.

'257 for 6,' he mumbled, 'Sachin Tendulkar can't be moved. Atherton's on his fourth over. It's brilliant . . .'

'Er, no. The pie . . .' smiled Amy, 'we meant the pie. The one that Mod and I made. How did you like it?'

'Oh it was *brilliant*. Well done both of you.' There was no mistaking his sincerity as he handed us a bone clean plate without removing his eyes from the screen. 'Any left?' We stared at each other's floury faces and crept out.

'Course it could have been camel dung,' said his sister, lovingly, 'and he'd have had the same reaction.

Ask him again when England's all out for 55.'

The following day, bright and early, I went to Marks & Spencer and bought three perfect fruit pies and a bottle of cider. Meanwhile the pear tree has bloomed and they're dropping like trousers in a farce. The way I look at it is this: sod 'em, let 'em drop – what else have they got to do?

Bored Games

I've discovered a remarkable fact which I shall pass on to you. There is something that women can do, that men can't. No, it's not that. And it's not that either. Lots of men can paint their toe-nails, eat an eclair and trash their sister-in-law at one and the same time. No. This is something much simpler, much weirder and much more profound. Something which puts us, as a physical breed, into a different stratosphere altogether. Something which involves a chair, a wall and a pelvis. Furthermore, it's something which Mickey Rourke couldn't do even if he had ten weeks to do it in.

Whatever your sex is, you begin by facing the wall and taking two foot-sized steps back. Then place a chair against the wall with the seat facing you and bend, straight backed, until the top of your head is touching the wall just above the chair back. Then keeping the head on the wall, lift the chair a few inches off the ground. Finally rise to a standing position holding the chair. *Voilà! Merci. Je vous remercie.* Easy as falling off a dog. If, of course, you are of the female persuasion. For it has to be said that whilst the fair sex are standing up chair in hands saying: 'Well, what's so clever about that? Anyone can do *that*!' their macho equivalents are still stuck at right angles, heads against the wall, bums akimbo muttering 'Hang on ... I can't get up. I mean ... this is ridicul ... Hang on – I must have taken *three* steps ... *Right*, lemme have another go ...' This is not an unfunny sight, and makes up for all those years of being arm-wrestled to the table in six seconds and getting smaller portions of meat because 'he needs the strength'.

This huge irrelevance was taught to me by my cousin Maurice a few Sundays ago, and it led to much discussion of masculine v. feminine differences, lateral thinking and the kind of puzzles which drive the puzzled into chewing the parquet. The one which always sticks in my mind is the man looking at the photograph who says: 'Brothers and sisters have I none, but that man's father is my father's son. *Question*: 'At whose photograph is he looking?'

Perfectly simple. Obvious even. Well, yes. Except I've known that puzzle for twenty years, forgotten the answer for nineteen of them, and have to start from scratch every time it comes up. (Answer upside down at end of chapter with a chair in its hands.)

And do you know the other one – now I'm really

swinging – about the father and son whose car is hit by an articulated lorry? The father is killed and the son badly injured and rushed to the nearest hospital for an emergency operation. The surgeon comes into the theatre, looks at the boy and says, 'I can't perform this operation, this boy is my son.' Explain and elucidate in not more than three sides of some foolscap paper.

As far as board-games are concerned the mere sight of them fills me with boardom. Years of relentless losing to an older, brighter brother made Monopoly, Totopoly and Cluedo the seated equivalent of cheerleading, guard duty or head banging in my list of least desirable activities. Trivial Pursuit always made me vaguely uncomfortable – something about the perpetual rethrowing of dice, the quicker to land on Entertainment and Literature and avoid Science and Geography at all costs, by everyone around the table, so that by the end of the game you know all there is to know about Michael Jackson's siblings and bugger all about Albania. Again.

Of course, for pure and puerile pleasure there's not a lot to beat 'shop snap'. This highly intellectual game probably invented by the Bloomsbury set or Frank Carson after a 'drink a yard of ale and toss your maiden aunt over a stile' competition, begins with a group of semi-plastered people (men, women, children and minah birds, whatever their pelvic girth, can play this game) sitting around with a pack of cards and an inane grin, and ends in the kind of mass mania usually associated with witch drowning or the inside of David Lynch's temporal lobe.

Are you sitting comfortably? Then get up and start again. Each person chooses a different shop i.e. A patisserie, a hardware shop, a grocery, a fish shop and, I'm afraid inevitably if you mix with the kind of person I do, a sex shop. Now for the tortuous bit. Armed with the knowledge of what shop you are, you proceed to play Snap. Yes. Normal Snap. Until the point at which two people lay down the same card and all hell breaks loose. Instead of saying 'Snap' you demand of the other person an item from their chosen shop – *before* they demand one from yours. This entails the simple act of remembering which shop all six people have elected to be.

I know it sounds easy, but I can assure you it's heinous. Not only can you not remember what shop they are but once you have remembered that it was a cake shop the only word which comes out of your mouth at full decibels, for some reason is 'Portrait! Portrait!' which you yell repeatedly, until the other person has finished ordering a pound and a half of chopped whiting and some crabsticks from you. And you, it goes without saying, were the sex shop.

Moderately normal, mildmannered people who teach schoolchildren or floss bridgework turn into frothing imbeciles before your very eyes. Some go completely silent but for the regular opening and closing of their mouths. Some speak in tongues saying 'gimp' or 'fallo fallo erk' in a higher and higher pitch until they faint and others physically grow in stature and point their fingers into the cornea of the person opposite bellowing, 'I want a large – large – largest biggest bargest large huge enormous great steaming big *wharrever it is you stock in your effing shop!*'

I bet you'd really love to spend an evening with me and my little friends wouldn't you? Admission free, do not pass Go, do not collect £200 plus VAT, please bring straight backed chair and person of male gender.

Answers: 1 He's looking at a photo of his son.
2 The surgeon was the boy's mother.
3 The writer is barking mad.

Innocent Parties

'I think we'll have a New Year's Eve Party this year,' I told my daughter, who'd come to join me on location during her half term.

'Great,' she said absently, 'I'll ask my class.'

'Well actually,' I added hastily, 'I wasn't thinking of your sort of party – erm – I mean, you know, your friends all want booze and cigarettes and messing about – I'd thought more of a *proper* party . . .'

She was looking at me strangely. I'd certainly got her attention.

'It's going to be an MDL party.'

'You mean people are going to come dressed as your initials?'

'More than that dear. MDL also means "Mutton Dressed as Lamb". A "come as you were" party – you know with jelly and cake and Pass the Parcel and Dead Lions when we're tired, which knowing most of our friends will be around 10.30.' (I didn't add 'Ducking for Apples' because it always reminds me of that wonderful Dorothy Parkerism: 'There but for one small typo goes the story of my life'.)

I could tell by the set of her brains that she was racking them. Finally she said: 'I've got a better idea. Why not have a "Come as your Favourite Noise" party.' This led to some minor hilarity and the confession that in the Sixties I had attended a 'Come As Your Suppressed Desire Party'. It was more than a little embarrassing for me, as I didn't have one. A desire, I mean. Suppressed or otherwise. Unless you counted getting a flat with a bedroom of my own, or never having to go down the Labour Exchange again.

In the end I went as 'The Wicked Lady'! I'd never actually seen the film – I just liked the sound of the words and I happened to have a black lace négligée in which I'd recently died (in more senses than one) in *Wuthering Heights* at the Palace Theatre, Watford. I swanned in, rigid with what I hoped passed for sex appeal, but apart from one brief interval sharing a dodgy stogey with a large American who wore his underpants over his tights and a large Star of David appliquéd to his T-shirt, (he'd come as SUPER-JEW), I spent the evening chatting to my former college mates about the state of show business and eating myself pear shaped.

My friend Sally, tells of a mother and daughter who went away on a holiday weekend, one of the attractions of which was a fancy dress dinner and dance. As they emerged from the lift, dressed to slay, the manager rushed over excitedly and said, 'Ooh, thank goodness you've bothered to dress up. We were beginning to think no one would do it!'

So saying he pushed them unceremoniously into a dining room filled with diners whose main concession to the art of fancy dress was a feather in their hair. Sally's friend's Mum had come as a blackbird. Her march to the table on huge padded yellow feet was something she'll remember, in a flushed fashion, at least once a day for the rest of her natural life.

Similarly or simianarily, *About Face* costumier Jimmie Dark told me he'd set out in the car for a costume party, discreetly dressed as a gorilla, and found on a foggy night in February, that he had to stop the car and ask a passer-by for directions to the house. Another friend went to a costume ball thrown by a frozen chicken firm called Sussex Sovereign Chicken. She decided to take the firm's name literally and went in her wedding dress, a red velvet fur-lined cloak, with an orb made from a plastic Easter egg sprayed gold, a chicken's head fashioned from a Balaclava helmet and yellow felt-covered flippers. She won first prize, but didn't get too many dances. Except the Funky Chicken I guess. When I last spoke to her she was planning to use the same outfit for a country and western costume ball, substituting a tan catsuit for the wedding dress. Her intention was to go as a barbecued chicken.

Most actors, who spend their lives dressing ridiculously, are more than happy to knock off in real life.

(Even as I write this I am wearing a shoulder length grey wig, broken veins, half glasses on a chain, several layers of ethnic gear and an awful lot of clanking beads, and that's just at 7.15 am in the location Winnebago). But those of you who've chanced upon these odd books in dump bins before will know that as a general rule, my husband and I will leap into fancy dress at the drop of a Fedora.

Indeed we do exactly that for our bi-yearly meetings with our accountant. It began as a joke to enliven his otherwise grey day, and has developed into a tradition as ritualistic as Christmas and almost as expensive. The first time he called we were in ball gown and tuxedo – not both of us, one each – and we've gone steadily down-market ever since. For the last serious discussion of our company earnings, the co-directors wore matching scarlet combinations, topped by Stars and Stripes underpants – well, overpants really – and baseball caps. Our accountant was impressed. He smiled. He even chuckled, called the meeting to order and got down to the important business of the day. Lunch.

My job at these meetings is to make the minutes, which I do with such verisimilitude that when read back they are funny enough to send accountants, pension planners and thespians crashing helplessly to the velvet pile. Actually, one meeting was videoed by our then secretary, Layla, as a response to the frequent question 'What's it like working for the Rosenthals?'. At the time we were in full Arab dress, with beards, yashmaks and many Marks and Spencer bags.

*

As for the 'Come as You Were' party – well, I found it hard to think of an incarnation I hadn't already played. Jacko's was easy. He spent his two years' National Service in the Navy – the only Jewish sailor they seem to have had, and that's another story shortly to be televised. The only other job *I'd* ever had was a week's work as a waitress in Bridlington. Consequently, we made several visits to our local party hire shop in East Finchley, and emerged as considerably more interesting-looking versions of what we once were. Leading Coder Rosenthal metamorphosed into Cap'n Jack and I was a waitress who wouldn't wait long, in a pink and white thigh length dress. Amy, who has a self-confessed desire to remain six years old and who knows *Peter Pan* by heart, was keener than mustard to get back into a baby bonnet and Adam, who spent at least one of his formative years wearing blue tights, a red cape and a large S on his chest, just raided my tights drawer. My mother refused to do anything but wear her most elegant knitted suit, so Jack wrote a label for her back which said 'I looked like this last week'.

The best thing about a fancy dress party is the entrances. After that, but for the odd shriek as someone who's been eating trifle on the terrace wanders in to meet someone who's been sipping Sangria in the study, the evening becomes a matter of how comfortable you are. Nobody knows more than I do the agonies of spending an evening bopping whilst disguised as a dressed crab or an inflatable hippo. But the standing at the door screaming 'I don't believe it! Jaaaaaack, come and look what Pikka's come as!' is unforgettable. In actuality, Amy's friend Pikka's costume was the wittiest of the evening – she wore a huge cardboard eye over her head through which her face appeared to one side of the pupil. She had come as 'the glint in her father's eye'.

A, shall we say, receding-haired Ivan suddenly had a mass of black, shiny locks and Denis King donned his old 'King Brothers' velvet jacket plus taped-on photo of the gang of three. Astrid wore her college sweater and hot pants which were practically pyromaniac. Lyricist Don Black dressed perfectly normally but for a blue knitted baby hat with earflaps and his wife, Shirley, who is what's known as the salt of the earth but in a very glamorous shaker, came with no discernible differences from her normal self, which for some reason made me laugh. What reason? Well it was because Don had made the gesture for both of them and Shirley was there to be just Shirley. Claire Rayner and husband Des were harking back to their flower power years, with Des *very* scenic in some sort of tan suede ensemble which made him look like a refugee from a Sherwood Forest that Calvin Klein used to inhabit. Actress Stella Tanner wore a lurex bodysuit and a hairpiece and eyelashes which looked like twiglets and Louie Ramsay had somehow fished out her somewhat elderly North London Collegiate straw hat. Lizzy and Roger were adorable schoolchildren, very public school, and their kids, Sarah and Mark, were giant nappied babies.

Most priceless award should have gone to two of our oldest friends, Bryan and Edith Butler, who had not only dressed up in full school uniform but had worked superbly hard at accoutrements. Bryan's 1939 satchel contained not only a squashed sandwich but a rubber frog, gobstoppers and stinkbombs and he had an Elastoplast on his knee, and his glasses. Barry Cryer, conversely, had made the minimum of effort. On his besuited back was a placard which read 'I've always looked like this'. We put him with my mother.

The food flowed and the wine did something similar and at midnight the motleyest looking guest list in town gathered around one King Brother at the piano. The kids held up the words:

'I saw the old homestead and the places I love
I saw England's valleys and dells
And I listened with joy
As I did when a boy
To the sound of the old village bells.
The log was burning brightly,
Through a night that could banish all sin,
For the bells were ringing the Old Year out
And the New Year in.'

The idea is, first, to sing it all together, then again with gestures, some nicely vulgar, on each line, then, finally, with gestures but no words. It's harder than you think and does add mirth to the proceedings. Denis Norden, who like Jacko is a man who'd prefer almost anything to standing up at a New Year's Eve Party with drink in one hand and a neighbour's wife in the other, was definitely having the best of times, I noted whenever I hobbled past, singing all the old songs at the top of his, and Barry Cryer's voice.

The prize for the most inventive costume went to Pikka and the prize for the most interesting costume went, of course, to Shirely Black for coming as – er – Shirley Black.

At 1.30 am, Miriam Margolyes and Susannah York arrived from a more fashionable down town party and stayed throughout the clearing up and out bits, nibbling things round the kitchen table. I was surprised but not displeased to see Miriam giving my mother a much needed back rub – but not as surprised as my mother was.

At 7.30 I'd been caught muttering 'Whose bloody idea was this anyway?' as I raced around throwing throwovers over bits of the furniture which seemed to have been masticated in the last year. 'Next time you hear me say "Shall we have a party" I want you to remind me how I feel right now! Murderous and hostile to everyone who's coming. *Not* that they will come – and look it's nearly eight and there's not a soul here! *God*, that's the bell and I'm not even dressed – Adam, get off the floor and answer the ruddy door. Who's had my mascara?'

At two o'clock I snuggled up next to the fellow who always seemed to be in my bed and said. 'Well it wasn't that bad was it? Everyone seemed to have a really good time, wasn't it nice to see all those old friends again. I really like giving parties, don't you?' The snores confirmed he did. Or didn't. Whatever you like, love. S'fine. G'night.

Later that same year was what we kindly refer as 'a milestone' birthday for Jack, who made it perfectly clear that he wanted it to pass utterly unnoticed. I tried very hard for, oooh, three or four minutes to abide by what he wanted, then thoughts of friends he hasn't seen for years intruded and my dialling finger started twitching. Before I could say 'don't shout at me I couldn't help it', the deed was done, caterers had been called in and friend Lizzy put in charge.

The day of his 'tieth birthday was a Monday, it was also the day after the second night of recording *Re: Joyce* for the BBC, the afternoon of the first read-through of my next play in Waterloo, and Rosh Hashanah, the first day of the Jewish New Year. I'm known for my timing. Fortunately, there are two of me and both of them are fond of delegating.

It was a quiet morning. Jack and Adam went to the synagogue and Layla and I had a good weep about some dilemma one of us was going through, then, stopping only to buy some baby clothes from ex-secretary Jo Kydd's baby shop, I drove to Waterloo for the read-through. The relief of speaking the words out loud was enormous.

At four o'clock I picked up friend Sandra Caron at the Young Vic and arrived home by five to prepare for the party. I realized I was tired and lay down on the bed whilst Sandra tried on various outfits in front of the mirror. At seven o'clock, Lizzy and 'Honeysuckle' the caterers arrived. By gum, that's the way to do it. I remained in my supine position and let them take the strain. At 7.45 the keener of the guests arrived, and from then on it was Jack's night. Wonderful, thoughtful presents and good, loving old chums. I'd managed to seek out the *Coronation Street* actor, Tommy Boyle, who had joined the Stables Theatre Company in 1970 as a stagehand and small part actor and who hero-worshipped Jack from day one, and actor John Shrapnel, who had been part of the Stables Company and the single source of most of our in-house laughter. He was rehearsing *Sophocles* at the Barbican, so bless him he *needed* a laugh. Gary Waldhorn arrived with, for reasons best known to himself, a large inflatable banana and I'd even got hold of Jack's old flatmate, director Les Chatfield, husband of Jack's ex-Granada secretary, Margaret.

It was all very last minute, but maybe that's why it worked. The greatest coup of all came through no plan of mine. Tommy Boyle had rung the day before and said, 'Listen, Mo, is the party still on, like?

'Yes, of course, Tom. Can you still make it?'

'Er, well, yeah, it's just that I'm meeting Besty for a drink before and, well, would it be alright if . . .?'

'Besty – as in George Best – y?' Jack and I had held hands through many Manchester Saturdays of what sheer genius really means and Jack had written

George's story for an American film company, which had, with whatever the sheer opposite of genius is, shelved it.

'So,' continued Tom, 'would it be alright, like? – I mean, we wouldn't stay long.'

I could've cried. Short of the entire Manchester United team coming out of an Eccles cake, there could be no finer gift for a lad in his prime. The Best.

Well, you could've knocked Mr Rosenthal down with a 1966 fixtures list. He wandered around with the biggest, daftest, most blissful grin on his glowing face for the whole evening, and when the toast was made he, most uncharacteristically, made an impromptu speech. Ad lib it was and spectacularly Talmudic, with a lot of pidgin Yiddish, he brought the house down and claimed he could have gone on for ever. A lot of singing then ensued and virtually no washing up. Now there's posh.

PS A few minutes ago my telephone rang and, as is my practice, I answered it. It was Paddy Burt, a journalist, asking if I would contribute to a series she was doing for *The Times* on entertaining at home.

'It's no good asking me, Paddy,' I told her, my pen still warm in my hand. 'I'm hopeless at it. I owe everyone in London and the Home Counties dinner and the only people I ever invite are the ones I don't owe a sausage roll.'

Then I started to think: 1991–2 New Year's Eve party, Jack's party, Denis' mother Win's eightieth party, Astrid's birthday lunch, Amy's party, visiting Americans' brunch, Rantzen/Wilcox/Nichols brunch, sleepovers every weekend (and the children's!) – hang on in there, Mo, you're doing your whack, if you have a brunch a fortnight you should have paid off your conscience by 1993. Meanwhile the entertainment at home is constant – see my son eat three bowls of cornflakes, several pints of milk and a bowl of sugar per evening, reading the packet throughout. See Jack attempt to explain fishballs (*again*) to Colombian Esperanza who, like Monroe, didn't know they had any. See Jack, the writer, in my absence attempt to write plays whilst his mother-in-law, up for the duration to 'help out', interrupts him every fourteen minutes with some domestic minutiae. See clenched writer finally say, 'Zelma. I am right in the middle of a script. Can you *not* bother me, unless it's absolutely vital. Really important. OK? I'm sorry, but I need to get on.' See Zelma acquiesce and disappear without a trace of huff and restrain herself for nearly an hour. Leopards and spots being what they are though, see her enter the study and stand there, hovering and staring fixedly at his back. She's there but she's not there, reads her body language. See writer look up, round and back. Hear writer sigh, put pen down and say, 'Yes Zel – it is *really* important isn't it?' See Zel quiver between truth and dare . . .

'Er, well, I don't know . . .'

See writer prepare for the possibility of the worst. 'Go on Zel – go on luv. Tell me. What's the problem?'

See wife's subtle mom reply brightly: 'Do you think this jumper goes with this skirt?'

See helpless (and colour-blind) writer subside on to blotter.

Home entertainment? In our day, we made our own fun . . .

2

Pro File

The Many Faces of About Face

The series of comedy playlets, *About Face* had been, like most first series, a bit of a hit and run affair – it was sometimes a hit, but would it run? I believed in it passionately and was delighted when, in November 1990, the *About Face* team reassembled for series two. Central Television had ummed and aahed about whether to risk a second series, but in the end they gave the go-ahead to director John Henderson. Not wishing to throw out both babies *and* bathwater, they transferred the location to Nottingham and told us to go ahead with new ideas and new scripts.

In the second episode of the second series, a group of us found ourselves water-marooned in a coach in Sherwood Forest. From 6.30 that morning, the rain had fallen down in torrents on the roof of our coach. I was playing a tourist guide, Keith Barron was my driver and confidant, and on every other day the sun had polished our pates and sent sun spots bouncing off the coach windscreen. Today's weather was a continuity nightmare, so, dressed and made-up, we sat in the coach and told jokes. It was a day to remember though the jokes themselves are long forgotten. Apart from one: the one where the man goes to the circus owner and says: 'I've got a fantastic act. I call myself 'The Great Semolini'. I come on with a fully-grown crocodile. I open the crocodile's mouth and I place my private parts in his mouth. The crocodile, of course, closes his mouth, so I pull back my fist, punch him in the eye, his mouth opens in astonishment and I take out my private parts and reveal them unharmed to the audience. They go wild!'

The circus owner, amazed by the man's description, offers him a job in the ring. 'You're on tonight,' he says, 'and you'd better be good.'

The evening the ringmaster announces: 'For the first time in circus history, the one and only daredevil animal act "The Great . . . Semolini"!'

On comes our man, with his giant crocodile. He opens the crocodile's mouth and places his privates in. The audience gasp as the crocodile closes his mouth. Semolini draws back his fist and bops the croc in the eye with all his might and the reptile releases him. Unscathed, Semolini shows his undamaged parts to the roaring crowds, says,

'Thank you, ladies and gentlemen. Thank you. And now you've seen my performance, I wonder is there any brave member of the audience who would like to try to do the same thing?'

Silence.

Then a tiny old lady in a tam-o'-shanter, in the back row, puts up her hand and calls out: 'Well, I don't mind having a wee go – but can ye no hit me so hard in the eye?'

There were many others, but fortunately for those of us with weakish bladders, the rain lifted and lunch was announced. A perfect morning. Three hours of laughter, wonderful company, no work and food in the offing. Sometimes I think I was made to work on munitions and be the life and soul of something.

During the week we filmed at Belvoir Castle and as film units always do, we took over the whole joint with people, props and paraphernalia. One shot, a difficult tracking shot from the entrance hall up to the tourist guide, Louise, leading fifteen or twenty tourists at top speed in and out of two doors, took almost an hour to set up. We rehearsed it several times then a hushed silence fell as everyone prepared for a take. From the tiled hall below came the First Assistant Director's shout. 'Settle down now, going for a take. And turn-over, sound running . . .' As the clapper-boy clapped 'Scene IV, Take 1', the clip-clip-clop-clop of a pair of sensible heels on tessellated tiles grew crisply in volume until they came clearly into vision surmounted by somebody profoundly regal.

'How *do* you do. I'm the Duchess. Very nice to have you here, everything all right?'

'Erm, yes thank, your gra–, your ladyshi–, you're very brave to have us here. Actually we're . . .'

'Not at all, we enjoy it. Would you care to come round for some tea after you finish your play?'

We assured her that we'd love to and she disappeared as she'd arrived, with immaculate timing and unteachable sang-froid.

Later that day, Keith Barron, John Henderson and I did indeed partake of tea in the Duke and Duchess's private quarters and it was country house elegant with dogs and wellies and other stuff from the pages of dentists' office magazines. That's what I love about this job. The perks.

Two other members of the *About Face* team, already firmly established as ace 'luvvies' were Dodie Ismay, make-up, and Jimmie Dark, costume. Dodie and I first worked together on the televising of *Long Day's Journey Into Night* starring Sir Laurence Olivier some nineteen years ago at the old ATV Rediffusion studios in Elstree. She was stunningly pretty with wide eyes and a short, blonde crop, and age doesn't seem to have withered her at all – the rat! The first day I travelled to Central TV Nottingham to do some make-up tests with her, I knew we were going to hit it off. We were trying on wigs, when an emaciated Sinead O'Connor clone wafted into the room, leaned against the counter staring at herself in the mirror and nasally intoned: 'I've just had my period, I've been pregnant for three months and I really want to be a video tape editor.'

It only took one look between Dodie and myself. We struggled with our faces for all of thirty seconds before we cracked. Dodie was a woman after my own funny bone. Single-handedly, she created six very different identities for one fairly undisguisable face, and for the next seven weeks we laughed when we should and even more when we shouldn't and sometimes when we couldn't any more.

Jimmie, an ex-dancer, is tall and elegantly thin, with a somewhat meandering pony-tail and loose stylish clothing. He has a way of describing an item which would never fail to crack me up entirely, as in 'we sewed the beads all around *what I call*, the neckline' or 'She had a very nasty condition around *what I call* the upper arm area' – as though *we* called it something entirely different. He also has an hysterical inside knowledge of the Hollywood greats, and once I got him going on the likes of 'your June Allyson' or 'your Doris Day', he would keep our eyes out on hinges for hours at a stretch. 'Didn't you *know*? Didn't you *know*? Oooh, I thought *everyone* knew that. Did it with everyone – athletes, removal men – ooh yes'. And one glorious day – 'Oh yes – she was well known for it. She was like a rutting pig! I thought *everyone* knew that.'

Apart from the humour, his costumes were inspired. He just brought them round to the house and they were perfect. Six characters, all utterly different, and every time he picked out the right selection of clothes. Or had them made-up. I've rarely had such a blissfully shop-free experience. The tourist guide outfit was made from scratch, as were all the ludicrous matching golf clothes for 'One for the Half' in which I played a golf widow who took up the sport and became obsessed by it. Acres of silly check culottes and Argyle sweaters arrived in boxes, and he somehow contrived to secure me the spiked shoes and logo'd socks not just for the play but for keeps! Boy have *they* been useful.

For the amateur opera singer – nice, suburban Anne in Carol Bunyan's *Requiem* – we just picked out my mother's favourite knits ('Oooh, she looked fabulous, dressed top to toe in Tricosa'), used them for the week and sent them to a good home. In Hull. For mad Mrs Firebrace, the animal rights liberationist, in Paul Smith & Terry Ryan's *Monkey Business*, we picked everything the Oxfam shop spewed up, and Jack's National Health hospital drama *Sleeping Sickness*, with its terminally tired junior doctor, was simply a white coat which could have doubled as the 'before' half of a Bold commercial.

Quite the cleverest bit of costuming was for Ian Hislop and Nick Newman's sharp satire *Briefcase Encounter*, a parody of the world of corporate business and tight-lipped, cowardly, unrequited love. We decided Deirdre, the busy career woman with the empty social diary, should be one of those women who had decided on her style and stuck to it relentlessly. One tailored jacket in five different fabrics, coupled with silk skirts and tops. Jimmie had the jacket run up in taupe gaberdine, dusky-pink worsted, mahogany tweed, black and fuchsia brocade (for that special evening look) and cream linen which defied creasing. Dodie coupled this with concrete sprayed hair, with a single grey streak which she carefully re-sited for every scene, and perfectly coordinating nails, lipstick, glasses and shoes – and voilà, Deirdre lived.

Simon Cadell was my co-star in *Briefcase Encounter*. One of the best things about *About Face*, after the pleasure of creating a character and a look with colleagues, is working with a new co-star each week. Most of the actors were people I'd admired but never worked with like Simon, Mark Kingston and Stephanie Cole. It's a bit like getting to know new people on a holiday. By the end of the week you feel as though you've known them all your life and possibly in a previous one. No wonder filming fosters fresh fancies. No, don't assume candid confessions are about to spew forth. Would I? Shatter your image, I mean? Neither would I tell you, and expect you to trust me again, that everyone was lovely, charming, delightful, talented and easy to work with. Because you would, and rightly, accuse me of bullshitting you.

So I'm here to tell you that Simon Cadell likes a nice Havana cigar at 7.30 am in the location Winnebago; that Mark Kingston is a migraine sufferer who eats six oranges at a throw ('Oranges, Mark!' I screamed. 'Oranges! one of the known causes of migraine!' 'I know,' he grins, 'but I love 'em.'); that

Keith Barron, as the coach driver, saying in reply to my, 'we don't want to rush Belvoir' (pronounced Beaver), 'Oooh, the last thing I like to do is rush Beaver', made it the rudest line ever spoken by man; that Martin Clunes is a laugh a millisecond, and that Bernard Hill is Bernard Hill, you'll know I'm trying to give you a balanced picture.

Director, John Henderson, who also directed and wrote some of series one, is as talented as he is tall – and he's six foot five in his Reeboks. How he completed six very different plays in very different styles in six weeks, whilst remaining calm, funny, good-natured, sensitive and inventive (a lesson in how good results can be achieved without bullying or temperament), I'll never begin to conjecture. (Right. That's it for the creeping section – Lipman's OK for work for the next year or so.)

Hendo liked his in-jokes. He's a great believer in background gags which are scarcely seen, except by the really fleet of eye. In *Briefcase Encounter*, he added a non-speaking motor cycle messenger. On his first appearance he had a bandaged arm and on each successive appearance he had a fresh bandaged area. In his final appearance he looked like the invisible man and walked like someone who's just been operated on for haemorrhoids. There was also a man mending a photo-copying machine with a *sink plunger*, two secretaries, one hidden completely behind a potted plant, the other behind a mountain of papers, and a poster on the back wall which changed from Jason Donovan to Prince in one single tracking shot. Sue Field, the continuity girl, went apeshit, but it made Hendo laugh and said something pointed about the fickleness of hero worship. During the Elizabethan banquet scene in *Tourist Attraction*, we had a background jester who was utterly depressed, a Japanese tourist knocking a Ming vase to the ground and two Merry Men knocking hell out of each other with breakable staffs at the bus stop. It's what Hendo calls 'substructure'.

In Jack's play, *Sleeping Sickness*, Hendo had a patient in the background in bed receiving grapes and the patient in the next bed receiving a coconut at which he gazed in a puzzled fashion. He also had a Schizophrenia Department sign with arrows pointing in two directions and a woman dressed as Queen Elizabeth I in Casualty with her arm in a sling. (He'd only suggested that as a joke and she'd had three wigs and God knows how many costume fittings.) There was also a scene in the junior doctors' revue rehearsal, where a life-sized plastic horse stood in the line-up.

My strangest memory of filming in a huge hospital in Nottingham was of the dirty corridors – subcontracted out for cleaning – and the number of disorientated people wandering round them looking for the right department (and these were *staff*), the general dowdiness of the wards, shortages of staff, huge cavernously empty wards and the overall atmosphere of terminal poverty. It was very bleak. It seems that all the things we've grown up to believe were our natural inheritance, provided we paid our taxes, can no longer be relied upon. Education, water, hospital treatment, employment, care of the old and needy, eye tests, dental care, student grants, and you can now add to that, the right to watch a decent game of football in your own living room. Nowadays, if you want new pencil cases in your child's kindergarten, you have to apply to the Council for a grant, mortgage your maisonette and attempt to interest Bob Geldof in a sponsored mud-wrestling match in Mile End Municipal Baths.

So here's the scene. Martin Clunes (the junior doctor) and I (the Registrar) are positioned beside the bed of patient, Roger Sloman, playing the discussion of his treatment, in between nodding off, standing up, after seventeen hours on duty. Hendo is beside the camera wearing his bum bag and attached computerized bleeper. (He's a divil for the gadgits is John.) This one is about three inches square and sports a tiny screen across which important teletext news can pass. Just as the camera is about to turn, he gazes down at it, freezes, picks it up, shakes it slightly and says quietly but with ferocity: 'She's out. My God. She's out. They've done it. Margaret Thatcher's *out*. They've bloody done it.' Thirty people crowded round three inches of microchip – no it wasn't a Tom Jones concert, it was cast, crew, staff and patients – and as the news of the great Conservative back-stabbing was confirmed, a cheer went up around that great endangered white elephant of a hospital which probably reverberated through the Channel tunnel to Calais.

There were people on that set who'd been five years old when she'd ridden to power on a redundant milk float promising clean brooms and fresh blood. We were stunned with the joy of it and short of conga-ing round the wards singing 'Ding, Dong, the Witch is Dead', there wasn't much we could do or say. So we carried on filming. With hope in our hearts and a nice, warm feeling in our spleens, poor optimistic fools that we were.

All my co-stars were fine 'corpsers', it's a sign of a good actor (as in 'good to work with') but none so fine as I. (I'm reliably informed that Paul Schofield, for whom I would cross the Gobi desert, blindfold on a Sainsbury's trolley, is positively wicked on stage and could reduce his co-stars to a butter mountain with one under-the-breath, out-of-the-corner-of-the-mouth-remark. If I didn't revere him for his talent, his ravaged beauty and his soul, I'd love him for that alone.) Half-way through the filming of *Briefcase Encounter* though, I think I peaked, corpse-wise.

The scene was a corporate business buffet at Wimbledon. Deirdre, in cream jacket and 'All Eng-land' coloured accessories, is filling a small plate with buffet delicacies whilst discussing business tactics, *sotto voce*, with Simon Cadell's unctuous area manager, Graham. The scene required us to move along the table, stop on certain lines to pick up our titbits and pass out of frame. It was going very smoothly until we reached the end of the long table and I happened to glance down mid-speech at the contents of Simon's plate.

It wasn't even funny. I don't know why I even mention it. It wasn't funny at the time. Nobody, least of all Simon, could understand why my voice began to quaver, my nostrils flare, my eyes to water and my knees to give with the effort of controlling myself. I was silently heaving like an old Austin Princess and, finally, tears streaming from my glasses, I sank to the floor of the marquee and lay there, convulsing, whilst everyone around, infected by my jollity, joined cluelessly in.

'What was it?' demanded Simon, when I began to wheeze to. 'What sent you? Was it me? What did I do? what *happened*?'

'It was ...' the heap was speaking.

'It was your ... your ... aaaah ... your ...' wheeze, '... aaaaagh, aaaaagh' and down I sank again in mid-explanation.

It took a while. Tea was served and boredom set in. I became embarrassed by the fact that I'd have to tell them this time, and not only would I subside again, but it wouldn't even be amusing when I got it out. You had to *be* there, looking at it from my point of view.

'It was ... what was ... on his pla-a-a-te ... waaagh!' and off I went again. Then, 'The thought of him trying to eat it, with a – a – drink in his other hand ... and ...' The producer was looking at me like Robin Williams looked at Robert de Niro in *Awakenings*. 'I'm so sorry ... I really am ... silly. I must be tired. *Sorry everyone* ... all this *time* ... sorry, it's just ... it was ... look at his plate ... he's got nothing on it but t ... t ... two beef tomatoes and an ... apple, waaaaaaagh ...' and off I went again.

A bucket of iced water and a slap around the kisser would have done it, but everyone was too kind – or too inhibited, or too scared of the insurers – to do it. Afterwards, I kept trying to explain why Simon's choosing the fruit and veg for Graham's self-regarding character had cracked me. I suppose he chose as someone for whom food was entirely secondary to deals, and for whom the intricacies of actually *how* to consume the food were an irrelevance. Whatever the reasoning behind it, it did for me. Tears before bedtime. Dodie had to completely renew my make-up before we could shoot again.

My favourite character of the six was the animal rights liberationist, Mrs Firebrace. She was a steely-haired, Indian printed, sandalled, vegetarian tyrant, who respected no laws she didn't have respect for. Accused by the Customs Officer of attempted cocaine smuggling, she 'stage-manages' him into releasing her, only to reveal that what she was actually smuggling through was a small chimpanzee. It was gorgeous, and I desperately wanted to do a spin-off series about her home life in the 'green belt', but Central TV didn't bite. They showed mixed feelings altogether about *About Face*. John brought in an impossible schedule on time and under budget. The previews were copious, interested and flattering, the reviews of each individual show were the best we'd ever had, including one by Peter

Paterson of the *Daily Mail* which almost brought a tear to my mother's eye it was so fulsome. Viewing figures began at eleven million and hovered around and just below, and public opinion was excellent. The powers that be weren't. Interested, that is. They did an *About Face*. If I'm honest with myself, I must say that the public are probably not keen on seeing an actor playing a new part each week. What they want to see is an actor playing the *same* part every week. Preferably, as John le Mesurier used to say, in the same suit. I'll *never* bloody learn that lesson, though. But, if my pride in anything I do is ever greater than my pride in those twelve often patchy, sometimes sad, frequently funny little playlets, then it will have to come before a pretty hefty fall.

Laugh Lines

One of the prime requisites for a long life in the acting profession is to have an extra layer of epidermis. A thick skin. This protects you against many of the slings and arrows of outraged forthrightness, not to mention cushioning you from dodgy corsets and flea-ridden tights. One of the other requisites is the ability to keep your most sensitive emotions as near as possible to the surface of your skin for easy recycling. Now if you detect a paradox here, you are not necessarily a person of genius. I think I can shrug off most criticism, both fair and unjustified (she lied) but the one that makes my teeth wince and my jugular pound is 'She is more of a comedienne than an actress'. Can any human being, of average skin depth, explain to me what this implies? Or why it applies to some comedy actors and not others?

If an entertainer stands in front of a mike and says

'A funny thing happened to me on the way to the visual reality centre the other day ... Now take my wife, no *please* take my wife ... So, I opened the door in my pyjamas, now there's a funny place to have a door ... He said to me, "I'm sorry to tell you but you've only got two months to live." I said, "I'd like a second opinion." He said, "All right then. You're *ugly*." No – listen – my mother-in-law's just had an operation, she'd had everything taken out and a new fireplace put in ...' Or, if they comment on the political situation, as in 'Did you hear what William Kennedy Smith said to the girl on the beach? No? He said, "If you don't let me do what I want with you, I'll get my uncle to drive you home."' Or (and here you need a passable South African 'iccent'), Interviewer to Eugene Terre Blanche: 'Now, tell me, Mr Terre Blanche, why do you have such a big grudge?' Terre Blanche: 'We'll, have yu seen the size of mah car?' Or if the comedian uses catchphrases like 'How tickled I am' or 'Yes, missus – ooh, nooo, *listen* – ooh, titter ye must!' or 'Oooh, you are awful, but I like it!' or tells long stories about British Rail sandwiches and Lyons individual fruit pies and embarrassing visits to the family planning clinic, then, I say, in my arrogantly humble opinion, they are what I can only refer to as comedian/iennes.

If, however, one rehearses and performs a character written by a writer, whose intention is to make the audience laugh, then, however comedic that actor's performance is and however much his audience is screaming and begging for breath and being carried out on life-support machines, I maintain that what that actor is doing is *acting*. He's playing the part. As closely as possible to the author's intentions. Just as he would approach *King Lear*, he's found the qualities within himself which most apply to the qualities inherent in the role, and he's brought them together. Often, of course, comedians can make glorious tragic actors. Less often does it work the other way round.

It still saddens me the way comedy is regarded as a secondary art form to 'acting'. As though one precluded the other. The oft-quoted sentence from Edmund Kean's death-bed, 'Dying is easy. Comedy is hard' (gloriously mis-quoted at a recent awards ceremony by Joan Collins as 'Dying is hard. Comedy is easy'), is a truism which few board-treaders would dispute. Laughter is a powerful weapon in the right hands. It can heal and wound, it can puncture and deflect, it can defend and attack. Things can be 'painfully funny'. You can laugh 'til you cry, you can be dying, screaming and bursting with laughter. Like I said, a powerful weapon. And a pretty powerful feeling when one is up there causing it, controlling it, conducting it.

I'm not discounting the writer's contribution, should he be different from the performer, but if he chooses the medium of performance art rather than the novel to tickle our ribs, then the onus is largely on the actor. In comedy, the actor must retain his character and tell the story of the scene truthfully whilst keeping an eye and an ear ever open for responses from continually changing audiences. This is a juggling act which actors in serious drama don't have to face. In serious drama the audience is a voyeur, not a participant, a silent contributor like the stage managers and the men in the flies or the house manager. How much simpler then, to concentrate on the job in hand.

The bias will never stop, of course. This year's Oscars looked like the 'Serial Killer of the Year' Award. I've nothing against Anthony Hopkins achieving recognition in the role of Hannibal Lechter. His was a marvellously chilling psychopath and I hope it's not just a showbiz rumour that he took to sitting next to ladies in the cinemas where *Silence of the Lambs* was playing, turning to them half-way through and, with a pleasant smile, saying 'Are you enjoying the film?' Of course it was, in truth, a film with a flaw as big as the Hammersmith Palais: why didn't they remove his teeth? Huh? One shot of Valium, one dentist with a death-wish and Hannibal's your uncle – the worst he could have given you was an unpleasant suck.

But where were the comedies this year? Where are they any year? Where was *When Harry Met Sally* the previous year? Where are Mel Brooks' and Woody Allen's Oscars and the *Naked Gun* and *Airplane*'s Oscars? Where was Chaplin's 'til he was too old to walk up and get it? Is it enough to expect Billy Crystal to host the ceremony each year yet never appear as an actor? Once again, it's as if the two processes were different. It is accepted that a political bias goes on in all awards ceremonies, witness their fear and loathing of Spielberg and Streisand, but a comedy prejudice? Well, yes. As though entertainment and enlightenment were somehow not enough. Too light for the heavyweight prize. The *ideal* candidate for the big time prize would be an actor, preferably himself a recovered alcoholic, playing a deaf, dumb, blind and profoundly disabled Mafia killer, who somehow gets the girl. Infallible. Oh, and if it's a British film, it should have period clothes, floppy-quiffed actors in white, a rented villa in some sepia-tinted isle, some heavily repressed sexuality and a leading lady who's 'somebody famous's' daughter.

The last awards ceremony I attended was a very surprising affair. It was the Olivier Awards and Jack and I were guests of The Theatre of Comedy. I decided to 'go for it' costume-wise and looked up some designs by a young man called Neil Cunningham. They were very forties, very beautifully drawn, very Hollywood retro, very *me*. He came over bringing a large piece of black velvet embossed with sprays of gold flowers and said, 'I've been wondering what to do with this'. The resulting high-waisted dress, gold blouse and jacket was a creation one could have called, if one was of a ludicrous bent, torreadorable. I felt good in it. Particularly when Kathleen Turner came skimming across the floor of the Grosvenor House Hotel to say, 'That dress is gorgeous, I've been dying to ask you where you got it all night'! I couldn't wait to get home and get on the phone which, I'm sure you know, is *totally* out of character.

The ceremony was held in the Dominion Theatre, an ex-cinema in the Tottenham Court Road. Everyone had instructions to be seated by 7.15 and at 7.35 we more or less were. Then followed at least eight, I would have thought, important awards, presented by the likes of Dame Judi Dench and Sir Ian McKellan, the latter, bringing the house down with his one-liner, in the wake of the Jason Donovan v. *The Face* case, 'I've tried not to bump into Jason backstage because I didn't want anyone to think I was straight.' All this was before the cameras began to turn. Diana Rigg, looking coolly elegant, did the intros very professionally. Then after half an hour, we, the audience, were told there would be a break of twenty minutes whilst the video tape was edited for tonight's 'live' transmission, and perhaps we would like to walk about, chat to friends or take a drink at the bar. All three thousand of us.

The twenty minute break took almost an hour and when the ceremony recommenced the audience's mood was unattractive. The actors who presented the prizes were deprived of their usual job of reading out the nominees on the grounds that often the names were too difficult to pronounce, i.e., 'And the nominations are: Zofia Abkgniewyskaya of the Pfganskorovitch Assembly of Hohenzollern Sigmaringen in *Gybroflos dsark a pzjunt* or *Wife Begins at Forty*'. Instead an electronic sounding voice took over from the presenter and listed the names smoothly and fluently. Or that was the idea. In practice what you got nine times out of ten was 'Good evening (one line joke courtesy of Barry Cryer) and here are the nom ...' loud distorted sound from electronic screen, deafening static boom and: ''igel Hawthorne for *TheM* – '*adness of George III*, 'obert Lindsay for ...'. This happened more times than it didn't happen, leaving the presenter pink and loose-jawed and our host and hostess for the evening white and clench-buttocked. And these are performance awards, given by the *industry*. I mean, you expect cock-ups at the school prize day or the Miss *Croydon Advertiser* awards, God knows, you stand there and *long* for them, but this is done by professionals, for professionals, to boost the profession. Or is it? Well, actually, no. It's not. Not anymore. It's done for television. It's making something very 'in' and possibly esoteric, palpable for the masses. As though the masses are not intelligent enough to appreciate theatrical honours because the bulk of the watchers will never go near the theatres in question. Well, there may be some truth in that, let's face it, a single broadcast of 'The Archers' on Radio 4 will reach more people than a year's run of *Phantom of the Opera*, but does a stagily visual event have to be televisually staged?

The awards for supporting performances and design and choreography and other integral parts of the nominated shows were excluded from the TV show, presumably on the grounds that choreography is too boring a department to interest the 'Bob Says

Opportunity Knocks' audience at home. The show was then tightly tailored around the advertisement breaks and the showstoppers are seen by you at home less as a theatre event than as a pop video. We in the auditorium were charmed, during a relentless number from 'The Blues Brothers', to see a video-clutching cameraman leap up on to the stage in front of the lead singer, wave and wiggle his camera up and over and round the singer's torso like a geiger counter, then scurry back down his hole like a guilty wood-louse. This drew the largest laugh of the evening, but you lot didn't see it.

Then there were the excerpts themselves. I mean there is a natural butter mountain of musicals on the West End shores, and a complementary quarry of straight plays, but your average Olivier Awards viewer could be forgiven for thinking they were watching the *New Musical Express* awards or, indeed, their teenage daughter's end of term review. The most successful play, *The Madness of George III*, starring Nigel Hawthorne, as part of the National's repertoire, only plays for three nights every second Michelmas week in any month with an R in it, and is totally sold out anyway, and the other award winners, *Becket* with Robert Lindsay and Derek Jacobi, and Martin Sherman's wonderful *When She Danced* have already closed. (Shomething wrong shomewhere, shurely? Ed.)

Of course actors don't stay in shows, even hit shows, for longer than six months these days. We can't really afford to be off the telly for much longer than that or else we lose our theatrical clout. Judy Holliday played *Born Yesterday* for four years. Derek Nimmo played *Charlie Girl* for seven! He still holds the record for the most performances in a day. It seems he was filming with Richard Widmark and Topol forty kilometres outside Madrid. The filming went over, and Derek was due back in London to play in *Charlie Girl*. He filmed from 7 am, then caught the noon plane back to London where he rehearsed his TV show *All Gas and Gaiters*, drove back to the Adelphi Theatre for the evening show of *Charlie Girl*, changed out of his costume in the car and flew back to Madrid to be on the set the following morning. (Those of us who've watched him do a matinée and three separate cocktail parties before the evening show, followed by dinner at the Garrick Club, will not be surprised by this story.)

So, television is feeding the theatre with actors whilst starving it of playwrights. Meanwhile, films on video and TV are luring the public back into the cinema. Films largely directed by directors who've cut their teeth on TV commercials and served no apprenticeship in either theatre or films. The rogue male in all this scramble for supremacy is radio. Radio which, of all the arts, is for me possibly the most visual, and which has fallen from grace to antiquity in a matter of half a century, has suddenly begun to feed everything. Yesterday's radio 'News Quiz' is today's *Have I got News for You*, likewise 'After Henry' and 'Whose Line is it Anyway?' This I regard as the only flicker of optimism in a demoralizing overall view of the media.

I know I said TV was starving the theatre of playwrights, but the playwrights are actually 'series-wrights' because there are virtually no plays any more, and our best writers are cottoning on that it's far less gall-bladdering and far more lucrative to write one episode of *Inspector Morse* than to give birth to a stage play, have it delivered by a theatrical paediatrician, fostered out to a small out of town operating theatre, have the whole surgery re-set in London and watch the poor corpse being flushed down the plughole by the critical equivalent of *The Lancet*.

Times were when you could switch on *Armchair Theatre*, *Saturday Night Theatre*, *Play for Today*, *Play of the Month* and see, well, a *play*. With a beginning, a middle and, if you were lucky, an end. All on the same night. With no break except for a quick scurry to switch on the kettle during the Finlay Currie/ Esme Cannon rural sub-plot. Nowadays if you want to know the outcome of the bank manager and the colleen's assault course or whether the make-up artist ran out of crêpe skin during *The Camomile Lawn*, you have to practically lay in thirty-two tins of corned beef and enough Andrex for a siege and go to ground for the duration. The lure of the mini-series. A paper-thin storyline stretched over far too many hours. A play, without the script editor's blue pencil through it, lasting long enough to fill a suitable overseas slot and thereby recover its budget.

I'm not talking *serial* here. Serial is different, a more leisurely way of telling a tale with cliffhangers and pounding chords. I'm not old enough to admit to remembering the BBC's *Little Red Monkey* with its sombre warning: 'Parts of this programme may be unsuitable for children or for people of a nervous disposition.' That was the bit through which my brother and I did our ambulance siren impersonations.

Of course in those days one had nothing much else to do but stay in and rapturize over the TV serial. Let's be honest, we *still* don't have much else to do, and yes we *could* video each episode – but *when do you watch it*? I'm asking you. In the middle of the day? Too guilty. I should be writing this ruddy book. In the middle of the night? I'd set off the alarm and most of Muswell Hill Police Station would be watching it with me. Early evening? When *Neighbours*, *Home and Away* and *The Bill* are on? Do me a favour. I want at least a nodding acquaintance with my children – until they publish their *Beattie Beat Me With a Jar of Bortsch* novellas.

So what's my beef? And is it over-done? My beef is that if you really don't give a whelk's jockstrap *Who* done it, and if the sight of one more glassy-eyed and still twitching corpse, batty local yokel or world weary detective with a hidden hurt, an unusual car and a penchant for Proust makes you swallow your tongue, then it's probably time to return your cathode ray tube to Radio Rentals and take up orienteering. Similarly, if your idea of a really good laugh is something other than a silver-toupéed Tory sharing a house with a rabid pinko/a black doctor with a bigoted white plumber/or a pneumatic blonde shepherdess with a gay rabbi, then join a video club and start at the very beginning with Buster Keaton and work through to Diane and Michael.

3

Personal Phial

Mid Life Cry Sis

'You must be prepared to be very patient, Maureen,' said my drama school principal, wrinkling his already wrinkled face into contours of concern, 'because you won't really come into your own until you're forty.'

It was 1967, my nineteen-year-old eyes filled with badly concealed tears and in spite of every Judy Garland film I'd ever seen, I resolved to give up acting immediately and take up, at best, typing and at worst marriage. Forty! Was there such an age? Forty meant support tights and roller sets and evenings where the men played cards at one end of the room and the women talked of millinery at the other. Blearily I thanked him for his advice, tottered out into the dusty warmth of the Earls Court Road and instantaneously blanked out his prediction for the next twenty-one years.

Five minutes, a few jars of moisturizer and several hundred meatballs later, it was 1986. It was spring. It was the Year of the Dog and I was starring in *Wonderful Town*. My first musical. I embarked on a feverish campaign of vocal and physical exercise that would have put Arnie on amphetamines.

I spent my fortieth birthday doing eight shows a week, twice on Saturdays and Wednesdays, and I can't recommend it strong enough as a means of ignoring the onset of middle age. Try it. All you need are eight young chorus boys, a revolving staircase, a thirteen piece orchestra, a town full of tourists and an awful lot of chutzpah.

Of course the real revelation of crossing the dateline, is that in your mind's myopic eye you stop ageing at twenty-four, and whatever evidence the overhead lighting on the Marks & Spencer mirror reveals, you remain that slim, earnest, questioning, confident young thing. Witness the phenomenon of bringing home your first baby from the hospital. The sudden hysteria of responsibility for this fragile tyrant, when you've scarcely begun to accept responsibility for yourself. You look down at 6lbs of pink fledgeling and it looks straight back saying 'I've got your number, Matey. Unskilled labour if ever I saw it.' You may bluster your way through but you know as well as baby that you are seriously under qualified for this post.

When did I last feel mature enough to deal with my son's teacher, my doctor, my hairdresser, my plumber or anyone foolish enough to be in my employ, without tears and abject grovelling to their face and accusations of total mendacity to their backs?

In shorts, the child becomes no further from the man, pardon my sexism, and we're mostly just actors playing grown-ups in a ludicrous farce, raising our hopes and dropping our trousers with Rix-like regularity.

Recently, Julia McKenzie and I had lunch with our respective spouses to celebrate her birthday. Now, between the four of us we clock up well over 200 years and our sell-by date is perilously close. However, we all confessed to the same feeling of shock when confronted by indisputable proof of our longevity, i.e., our gums, our children applying for a driving licence, or the news that Helen Shapiro is celebrating thirty years in show business.

'I suppose it really hit me,' mused Jack, removing his glasses so that he could see something, 'when I was walking down a corridor in some American hotel, with my young research assistant. Limping towards us was a fat, crumpled and very ethnic looking old man with a young micro-skirted blonde by his side. God, I thought, how ridiculous that man looks – if he could only see himself. It was only after another fifteen feet or so that I realized that we were walking towards a mirror.'

All the same, when I see a marvellous, indomitable old lady like say Dame Freya Stark, or study Joyce Grenfell, or meet a Hannah Hauxwell, I'm aware that what endears and propels me towards them is the child, still so evident in the grown up. A child-like enthusiasm which I find infectious and reassuring.

When I spoke at the Cambridge Jewish Society this year, I was immediately fazed by the extreme youth of the students. Why I should have expected otherwise may faze *you*. After all, my daughter will be an undergraduate in a few months, though I still have the irrational desire to follow her at a discreet distance every time she goes for a bike ride. It's not easy. On the one hand she tells me she's never going to grow up, and accordingly has willed herself to stay 5'3" and a size four shoe. Her fifteen-year-old brother, who has no such hang-up, overtook her in height some years ago and his feet are like coracles. On the other hand I'm not to treat her like a child, interfere, make 'chicken's tochas' faces when she's on the phone for 180 minutes or criticize anything about *her* personally or any of her friends.

Also, I must never again embarrass her as I did after Eddie Kulukundis' birthday luncheon by turning up in a black cab at her school with an orange helium balloon tied to my head. This is *not* the way mothers behave, she tells me, maternally.

How would *I* know? I'm so used to being embarrassed by mine that I'm anaesthetized. So used to sentences such as the one she threw me telephonically after she'd travelled to Brussels by overnight ferry to stay with my brother, 'I say, Maureen, you know that girl I slept with on the way over to Brussels – well, she's ever so nice and she's going to show me round NATO.' Once you know and love her it rolls off your back like a duck but, even for me, that one took a couple of minutes to sort out. I'm being utterly patronizing, don't tell me, I know. Fortunately, now *I'm* a mother, it cuts both ways. Last week I had tickets for the Shakespeare in Regent's Park.

'Adam,' I said, 'would you like to come out with me tomorrow night?'

'No thanks.'

'Well! That's *very* nice! I've got tickets for *A Midsummer Night's Dream* in the Park.'

'Oh! Sorry. Yes. I'd love to. I thought you meant to go to Pullens.' (Pullens, for the non-initiated non-north Londoner, is the school uniform shop in Temple Fortune.) The poor child thinks that's the only place I ever *take* him to. He's not far wrong.

Similarly, a conversation with him about a week-end break turned into a music-hall routine.

Me: Adam, I've been talking to Uncle Geoffrey in Brussels – how would you fancy us joining him for a couple of days in the mountains at Abondance?

Him: Er. No thanks.

Me: (to his father in a hiss) That child is ruined! I ask him if he'd like to go skiing with Geoff and me and he turns me down flat.

It was only after I returned from work a couple of hours later that his father told me the reason for his son's outright refusal. *He* thought the sentence went 'How would you fancy joining Geoff for a couple of days in the mountains at a barn dance?'

Under the circumstances I guess 'Er. No thanks' was mighty polite, paternal even. Get out the knitted throwover, Maureen, put your teeth in a tumbler and rock on. I've already reached the stage where I've forgotten whom I've rung by the time they pick up the phone: 'Hi – er – it's me, Maureen . . . er – how's things? Good, good, fine – and how's er, how are you, er both . . . still in the show? You're not in a show? Nooo, I didn't say *show*, I said – *so* – so, er who, I mean how *are* you?'

When I visited the Nightingale Home for the Aged, I met a very dear old man who whiled away his time making and painting small Jewish gnomes. Shrugging, tailoring, beaming, bearded gnomes. I ordered *six*. Sometimes I gaze out my window at the five who haven't been decapitated by a football and think – I could do a lot worse than end up at a respectable age, sitting in a favoured chair, surrounded by admiring friends, doing a spot of lucrative gnome painting. It's what I've always fancied – a job with good prospects.

In actuality, aside from his timing, my drama school boss wasn't far wrong. At fourteen I looked forty. At forty I felt twenty. At thirty-eight, the *Guardian* congratulated me on my forty-eighth birthday. At forty-four, the *Sun* wrote: 'Lipman, forty-six, was quoted as saying . . .' On top of which the entire British public thinks I'm a sixty-five-year-old telephobic, who's has plastic surgery to appear on chat shows. Maybe maturing is for cheese and wine parties, not for real life.

It was shortly after my forty-fifth that I stopped in Hampstead to buy, on a whim, a mushroom crêpe from a crêperie stall. (Hampstead specializes in stuff like that. And candle shops and Moroccan Wall Hangings – but go try and find a nice tea-towel!) The crêpe was delicious and I virtually slurped it back all the way to the car. As I revved up, I noticed a vanload of men waiting for my space. I indicated that I was about to leave. To my astonishment the driver leaned forward and somewhat suggestively ran his tongue around his lips. Well! See Mother Maureen bridle and bristle and stiffen imperceptibly or even perceptibly! I shot him one of my most disdainfuls – a 3B as it happens – only to see the passenger seat occupant lean forward and join him mid-lick for more slow tongue turning. I was appalled. Or was I? Secretly, a little voice murmured 'well, I never did – there's life in the old girl yet' and I stole a coy glance into the driving mirror to check how I looked. Yes, you've guessed it. There was mushroom all round my mouth. It was quite embarrassing actually, although the occupants of the van seemed to find it hilarious. From now on 'crêpe' is relegated to blouses and necks where it belongs.

Trance'd be a Fine Thing

It had to be the coldest, wettest day of the year when my mother and I drove to the hypnotherapist in Hampstead, and the new parking restrictions had to entail a half a mile walk and the kind of pay-and-display techniques which could only be interpreted by a traffic warden with X-ray vision or an ex-member of SMERSH.

Why the hypnotherapist? Well – look at it this way – I have enough mental blocks to construct a muddle village, my mother has anxiety attacks which make *me* anxious and the hypnotherapist's PR had written me a charming letter suggesting I might be anxious to try it. Accordingly, I put on my fake fur, grabbed my simulated crocodile bag and set off in search of reality.

Mr Robert Farago of the Farago Clinic is a young Clark Kent-like American with trendy hornrims and a ready smile and, after consultations with my mother, he took the short straw and decided to deal with me first. I filled in a form citing my blocks and before I actually spilled off the form and began writing on his shirtfront, we decided to deal with the sleep problem first.

In reply to his casual question, I gave him a run-down of my bedtime routine. His eyebrows drew together and his voice was quietly incredulous.

'OK, so you're telling me that you give a performance of two and a half hours till 10.30, drive yourself seven or eight miles home till 11.00, eat a full meal with meat and two vegetables whilst entertaining your children, your mother and various houseguests from assorted corners of the globe till 12.30, drink a caffeinated drink, stimulate your brain reading through a script or an article until one o'clock then attempt sleep? Would that be right?'

I made my face suitably rueful as we agreed that as wind-downs go, this was winding strongly upwards. I would, at that point, have been happy to pay my money and relinquish the leather chair a sadder but wiser woman – but the treatment was only just beginning.

Mr Farago wondered if I would like to be taken down to a medium trance, slowly. The fanged face of a traffic warden imploded across my middle eye and I said:

'Er, no. If it's all the same to you, I'd like to go into a deep trance very fast.'

There followed some experiments to see if I was a

good subject. He suggested one of my hands became a magnet and the other a metal slab and we both watched them being drawn together. Then there was some light-fingered stuff involving an imaginary helium balloon and it seemed we were off. His voice was authoritative and his manner persuasive as he issued commands to my subconscious. My limbs soon took on an uncharacteristic slump but my brain continued to buzz. I tried to stop myself comparing his American patois to those self-help migraine types you inadvertently pick up at the health shop with the Evening Primrose Oil, the Tropical pic'n'mix, and the leaflet on do-it-yourself breast examination.

'Your mind is a deep pool within which all human endeavour dwells. Unlock the channels of that innnermost cavern and the river of life will pour forth, bringing peace and harmony and state of undreamed of bliss. Remember your destiny is within your own head.'

'So is my headache,' you growl, struggling with the desire to karate chop the tape recorder.

Right now, however, I was struggling with the concept of visualizing a place where I had been supremely happy. It didn't have to be a real place and I was to raise my thumb when I'd thought of somewhere. The first picture which came to mind was a somewhat clichéd desert island, replete with timber shack and palm fronds, and I was just about to raise my thumb when a ruddy great crocodile padded up the sand and forced me to change the visuals to the lyrical calm of the Italian lakes, over which descended the biggest black storm cloud you've never seen. I began to panic. OK, my bedroom. I'm happy in my bedroom. No, he'll think I'm agoraphobic – or nymphomaniac even. Now I was starting to laugh – control yourself – my thumb was twitching ... Oh God – Cornwall! That's it Cornwall. Lake House. The sloping lawn, the cedar tree, the hammock. Fine. I stuck a triumphant thumb in the air and resumed basic breathing.

Over the next few minutes, his authoritative voice talked me down to a state of complete relaxation. At his suggestion, I left all my cares and woes in a rucksack at the top of a flight of stairs – I felt the sun on my face, the weight of my limbs, the movement of the hammock, the gentle breeze running through the windows of my mind.

'I'm going to tark you down from twenny to zero and each number will take you into a deeper state of relaxation. Whenever you think of this magic place you will feel as peaceful as you do now – twenny, nineteen, eighteen ...'

I began to feel quite soporific ...

'Twelve, eleven, ten ...' I gave myself up to the persuasion in his voice ...

'Six, five, four ...' Parts of me which had been tensed since teething, unfolded ...

'Three, two, one ...' I was sinking, sinking, sinking, when 'CRASH' into my head, into my hammock, into my Cornish rhapsody came an insistent, familiar, familial sound ...

'Hellooo. Are you there? I don't mean to suddenly interrupt but it's your meter, Maureen . . . It'll be running out in a minute – I mean you don't want to unnecessarily get another ticket do you? . . . Hellooo? I say. It's only, you left it at eleven o'clock and . . .'

Fixing my practitioner with my most hypnotic gaze, I said, 'And there, in a couple of split infinitives, you have the story of my life.'

It wasn't his fault. It was mine. I'd made the appointment forty-five years too late.

As I beetled back through the biting rain towards my shortly to be hostaged Hondamatic, a police van sounded its alarm, alarmingly, to my left. I swerved and focused my spectacles on the dozen or so traffic wardens seated snugly inside, hands waving wildly, faces all pressed to windows mouthing 'Hello Beattie – how's your Melvyn?' In vain I tried to regain my trance-like calm, but the words 'piss off' seemed to bubble effortlessly to my lips with accompanying gesture.

An hour later I picked up Mother who appeared with rainhood, gloves, umbrella and all the other accessories which manifest themselves from within her handbag, and the broadest smile I'd seen in weeks. My God. It's worked. She looks happy. I mused. Oh ye of fickle faith.

She got in the car and said trimphantly: 'He's very good, isn't he? I enjoyed it. I never went to sleep though. Did you? I kept opening my eyes all the time and saying "I'm not hypnotized you know".'

I'm sorry. There are some challenges that stump even the mastermind. Small wonder then, that I picked up my *Independent on Sunday* to find that women are attending this clinic in order to increase their breast size. The *Tatler* journalist reported an increase of half an inch (per breast, I presume) after one session. And if it can do that for WOMEN – then every man in England must be leaping into his car. No wonder the residents of Hampstead are complaining there's nowhere to park.

Weight for It

On the subject of going topless, it's several months since the annual *vacances* – or in my case the fortnight I lost the skin off my nose, the Access card, the new Gotex swimsuit over the hotel balcony, several of my friends and most of my marbles – but with the labels still on my luggage, I feel that distance has given weight to my reflections.

Weight. How that word comes up, mixing memory with obsession. All right, so it just happened that I just happened to gain one and a quarter stone this year. A combination of an operation, a sluggish metabolism, a smug belief that my clothes had shrunk and a propensity to stuff my face like a Vietnamese pig. As the bottom of me ballooned and the face and neck remained stationary, I acquired the look of a freezer bag full of stewed fruit and well-meaning strangers in Debenhams and my mother began to tell me how well I was looking. 'Well' as in 'rounded', you understand.

It didn't bother me during *Re:Joyce*, my one-woman show, as the 50s dresses all had full skirts, but on the night of the Society of West End Theatres (SWET) awards, when the dress that my designer friend Ben Frow had sent down from Liverpool with a friend in a plain brown wrapper – the dress, not the friend – arrived. I tore open the parcel, mewing with anticipation and tried tying it on. The long and the short of it was that the width and breadth of the dress was somewhat less than that of the person due to present the hideous statuette later that day and the said hippopotamus's mother was forced to get gleefully busy with scissors, thimble and pin cushion. 'Shall I cut it right up the seam, then? Are you sure?' She grinned like Madame Defarge at the guillotine. 'Didn't you mention to Ben that you'd got so heavy?'

Very few people that evening at London's glamorous Grosvenor House were aware that the cool brunette cracking the wisecracks was wisely held together with double-sided tape and knicker elastic and that underneath the yards of bronze silk chiffon she resembled a piece of rolled and boned brisket.

Fade out, fade in, to a few weeks before the aforesaid holiday when Lumpy Lipman drags out the summer case and attempts to reconcile size 10 bathing suit with size 14+ thighs. Straight to Mundy Sports waddled I, for the purchase of two extra-strength Dyna-Bands in a last-ditch attempt to trim down what the bikinis wouldn't or couldn't constrain. Of course, once in France, after approaching the pool wrapped in floor-length camouflage and lying in one position for an unnaturally long period of time, I had a flash of inspiration and realized that it mattered not a toss that I resembled an elderly mozzarella, because no one in their right mind, which admittedly ruled out most of the clientele at our particular hotel, was going to spare me a microglance with all that freshly toasted, perfectly basted pert crumpet all around them.

Who would guess that the human breast could be so omni-faceted and so multi-varied? I realize that the male 'wedding tackle' is probably just as varied but, still, the exposed fronts of the Côte d'Azur – rows and rows of them, knee-deep and four abreast, if you take my meaning – fair makes your pupils protrude. And I'm a *girl*.

Unlike the Mayor of Cannes, I've nothing against nudity on 'tidiness' principles. Indeed, were I built like a whippet instead of like Clement Freud's bloodhound, I'd gladly, proudly, let it all hang out. I just don't think I could do it as *they* do – lounging in large chatty groups of business associates, or playing racquet ball.

Take the Italian connection on adjacent loungers to ours. Fascinating. All the women were considerably younger, deeper-voiced, and only slightly less be-jewelled than their husbands. Regardless of sex, all chests were bared – you could tell the difference, though, because the men's were, for the most part, hairier. They were all loath to get wet, but when they did they did it in groups, standing knocker-deep in the water chattin' Latin. I mean, I was under the impression that if an Italian man caught another man looking at his wife's breasts, the guilty man would be barbecued in a vat of *linguini alla vongole* and a stone would be carved 'in loving mammary'. But no. I pondered how the scene would play in a different location, say at the NatWest – all of them casually rubbing Piz Buin into their nipples while enquiring after their bank balances. Where would you look?

However, I must tell you that my worst confrontation with the human body came when I happened to turn on French TV late one night after a heavy *bouillabaisse* and far too many *frites*. I got the *frite* of my life. Fully fledged, audaciously obscene, ambisexual hard-porno on screen in my very *chambre*, and no doubt in my kids' *chambre* next door. Twosomes, threesomes, *gruesomes*! Featuring some of the nastiest and most single-minded specimens I've ever had the misfortune to ogle. And the pooɪ cameraman!

The next day the occupants of the Cannes beach looked playfully quaint. Puritanical, even. And pearshaped and thankful, I lay back and thought of England.

Chicken and Chippendales

'We're taking you out,' said my friend Sandra on the phone. 'A belated birthday treat. Thursday. Be in Joe Allen's restaurant at seven.' Then, peremptorily, 'Don't ask, it's a surprise.'

I'd already had my birthday treat to which Sandra hadn't been able to come. I'd organized it with my customary precision, i.e., I'd said to almost everyone I'd met in the preceding weeks: 'I've decided to go ten pin bowling on my birthday – wanna come?' Since they all said yes and since I'd then completely forgotten whom I'd asked, the guest list on the night was a shade arbitrary. For weeks afterwards, I'd start to tell the story of the bowling alley to people who'd interrupt with 'You asked *us* to come to that then we never heard another word! Charming!' This is the Lipman way to deep and lasting friendships – I may

publish something on the subject in the near future.
Like a haiku.

Thus it was that twelve understanding chums who
knew me well enough to ring a week before the big
day and say 'Is it still on?' and 'What do you *mean* is
what still on?' congregated at the Superbowl for
chicken in the basket, birthday cake and a couple of
hours of the stuff that requires the strong right arm
and the sweaty shoes.

There had been quite a lot of consultation with
the management beforehand. Son Adam, at fifteen,
wasn't allowed to eat in the bar on account of his
parents didn't conceive him three years earlier. So, a
special eating place was to be designated. My heart
spiralled downwards when six of us burst out of
Jack's car to be shown proudly, by the manageress,
to the special place. The photocopying room. There,
on two adjacent Formica tables were twelve sad little
paper hats and a bottle of sparkling white. No, fair
do's, I was born in 1946 and it was my forty-sixth
birthday and I intended to push the trawler out.

Friends arrived in various states of bewilderment.
Louie Ramsay had given herself a good hour for the
twenty minute journey and had just made it. Julia
McKenzie had abandoned her car in somewhere
called Ickenham. Everyone she had asked for directions had never heard of the Superbowl and only
spoke Hindi if they had. Lizzy and Roger, old hands,
had no trouble at all, so why on earth hadn't we told
them to pick up Louie who lived ten yards down the
road from them? The hosts, who had discussed the

possibility of missing the left hand slip road to turn right off the North Circular, had missed it in mid-discussion, and were in a post-domestic sulk. It looked like being a little cracker of an evening all round.

Still there's really nothing like a glass of warm sparkling wine with friends to relieve pre-match tension, and when the chicken arrived in its basket, the mood lifted enormously. Have you ever asked yourself why the chicken has to be in a basket? It's just a drumstick and some chips, isn't it? Yet, like 'Boeuf en cocotte' or 'salmon en croute' its name derives from the vessel in which it stands. Why not chicken in a coal scuttle or chicken in a slipper? If the basket were edible I could understand it but when did you last cry 'oooh look, lamb chops on a *plate*!'?

Adam, who is growing, ate his in nine seconds and re-ordered, to the astonishment of the rest of us who would have willingly paid him to eat ours. He wouldn't have taken it, since he has an aversion to food which anyone has touched. I think the real attraction for him was that it was a utensil-free meal. A hands to mouth job. Consequently, no bulging-eyed and gizzard-necked looks from the gorgon one can only describe as his mother.

One of my birthday cards showed a Hollywood producer by the poolside saying 'I'll have your people call my people and we'll do cake.' Well, cake was done and mouths were wiped with damp hankies and suddenly it was time for the heavy duty part of the evening. Two teams, two alleys, twenty-four shoes and a lot of serious sticking of fingers into different sized ball holes. Later, we stood in a largish circle having the vagaries of the electronic scoreboard explained to us by a charming young woman in 'Superbowl' costume. Then Adam explained it all to us again and we were off.

Now, there are natural bowlers like there are natural ballroom dancers. I am neither of these and my daughter is even less so. Carrying the lightest ball as though it was a dead horse, she tottered up to the starting line where the ball appeared to fling *her* before dribbling ill-naturedly into the left gully. Helpless and pink, she repeated the process for her second shot and with a fine sense of fairness it dribbled into the right gully.

It was quickly discovered that all the women had bad backs. In fact, out of twelve people, seven of us were clients of Barry the Harley Street osteopath, and two more visit his rival in the same street. Julia's back was in fact freshly put back that very week. Limping, creaking and wincing, we heaved our heavy balls at ten ninepins. This would not have been Barry's strong recommendation. Still, smashing hell out of them and coming back to a triumphant roar of approval from our fellow sufferers, took him right out of our minds.

Louie, who plays Inspector Wexford's wife in the Ruth Rendell series, was deceptively clueless. She managed to send the ball plodding down the aisle so slowly that we wondered if it was actually moving at all, but with an accuracy of direction which was unerring. The pins were so complacent that the ball was never going to reach them that they collapsed more from shock than from the impact. They just subsided, like pastry.

Astrid, being American, had her own bowling shirt. With her name and team on it. She'd been waiting twenty-one years for the opportunity to wear it. I can't remember how she bowled 'cos I was so bowled over by what she wore to do it.

Denis and Roger, on the other hand, had enormous power, as did Adam although his tendency was to list to the right and, along with Jack 'the men' tended to get strikes and spares every time. My style is to knock down eight pins on the first throw and miss the remaining two on the second. This in itself was not funny, but the bodily lurch as I willed it westerly with most of my moving parts apparently looked mighty quaint. If you like quaint things that is.

One time late in the first game I was approaching the line at the same time as Amy. 'Just visualize them all dropping down,' I told her. 'Like in tennis – use your imagination and let your arm just follow it.' A second later I bowled a particularly average shot and heard a giant shriek of joy followed by sustained cheering. Shyly but proudly I turned around to accept it, only to see a small glowing pink face in the next lane and across it a grin as big as Paris. It was Amy. She'd struck. In one. If there is a God of Bowling he'd been keeping score.

By the end of two rounds we were all merry as

March hares, planing regular teams and deciding on our logo.

Back home there was pink champagne and the prettiest birthday cake, iced in white and the palest pink hand-sculpted flowers by Deirdre Kennedy's mother. Deirdre had organized a recent fund-raising lunch in aid of the genetic disease, Friedreich's Ataxia. It was the most perfectly organized charity event I've ever spoken at, and coming, as it did, a few days before my birthday, they'd even thought of making me the cake.

OK. I've explained how the cake came about, now I'll explain why nobody came back from the Superbowl to eat it chez nous. Our aged legs wouldn't take us. Two games of ten-pin bowling and all twelve of us were gaga.

Yawning and creaking we went home promising to congregate around our table on Tuesday two nights later and thus prolong the festivities. This was an incredibly verbose and diversionary way of telling you that Sandra Caron didn't come bowling on my birthday.

Jump cut to Thursday night where, dressed in fashionably crumpled beige linen and pearls, I picked up Astrid in Hampstead to drive to Joe Allen's for a pre-surprise supper.

'Are we still seeing *Basic Instinct*?' she casually enquired.

My animus was instantly animated. 'Really?' I grinned, somewhat lasciviously for one dressed in so much worm spun fabric, 'Ooooh *great* – I didn't know we were – she told me it was a surprise.'

Astrid jumped guiltily. 'Oh shit, sorry. I guess I shouldn't have . . . Trust me – mouth of the month.'

'It doesn't matter,' said I. 'I'll just pretend I don't know. Oh *great*. Jack would never have gone with me.'

'Nor Denis,' said Astrid.

'Do we get to see Michael Douglas's willy?'

'I don't know. Do we really *want* to see Michael Douglas's willy?'

We decided we didn't. It was the socio-political sub-infrastructure of the film which we were basically, instinctively, interested in. Yeah? And ice-cream doesn't melt and Warren Beatty's a virgin.

I thought Sandra was rushing us just a little through our potato skins and sour cream, and as we left it did occur to me that the Strand wasn't very well served for cinemas, but the penny only plummeted as we rounded Russell Street and saw hoards, coach loads, warehouses full of lycra'd women oozing into the Strand Theatre. The pavements were dizzy with potential lust, the air was charged with mischief, and high in the sky, in neon as high as a follicle-free thigh, was a twenty foot side of beef in a bow tie and two thrilling, chilling words, 'The' and 'Chippendales'.

'Oh God. You didn't?' My, erstwhile, chums were giggling in a superior sort of way, indicating that both of them were in on the ambush and *Basic Instinct* was a masterly addition to the plot. 'Of course,' I groaned. 'Jeremy got you the seats, didn't he?' He had, the swine. Jeremy Adams, company manager on *Re:Joyce*, was now pitting his considerable talents on a similar evening with nineteen more members (so to speak) of the opposite sex. If I didn't die first, I'd kill him.

It was the walking in that did it. I got past the satin jockstraps sized small, medium and 'Oh my God', OK, but the entrance into the front stalls in full light stoped me in my tracks like a sheep at a dip.

'Come *on*,' bleated Sandra. 'What's the matter?' She looked uncomprehendingly at the cowering load of linen that was me.

'It's alright for you,' I hissed, as the programme seller tried for the third time to sell me twelve square inches of glossy torso, clutching, for some obscure reason probably best known to Erica Jong, two dead fish on a hook. 'They don't *know* you. They won't all be pointing and making bbrrr-brrr, brrr-brrr noises and asking you to sign their husband's jock strap! I mean can't we wait 'til it's dark?'

The next fifteen minutes until the show began were something over which I should like to draw seven veils. Maybe eight. Finally, blissfully, the lights went down and I looked up.

Well, girls, if you've never tried it, don't knock it. This is a professional, well performed, well sung, well hung ... *together* (fooled ya!) show, and just about every female fantasy is catered for. What you see is what you don't get, i.e., innuendo, bulging biceps and fun buns, and the promise of something

you are unlikely to get when you get off the 43 bus
and go home to 'him indoors'. *No* full frontals
whatsoever. Just G-strings, a bit of simulated thrust-
ing and whole numbers given over to pectoral oiling.
The lads are, fortunately, not blessed with much
sense of humour or irony, so they go through their
horny routines as though they really mean it, and the
best ones seem – like the best female strippers –
almost innocent.

It's the audience who are the real focus of attention. Like most successful TV programmes nowadays, it's the public who are the stars. Famous for
fifteen minutes. After all, what is 'Karaoke' but a
turn around the piano featuring the shyest member
of the family, egged on by all the others. Bring me
your holidays, your worst moments, your weddings,
your singing spaniels and we will guarantee you
instant recognition in the dry cleaners the following
morning.

That's the secret, these girls are out on the town,
moussed, teased, shiny legged and raring to be
noticed. From the moment the curtains part their
presence is omnipresent. It's circus meets music-
hall via pantomine. 'Oh no he didn't! Oh yes, he
did!' 'Now is there any little girl out there who'd like
to come up and help Uncle Gregg to do his little
trick?' 'Yeeees! Yeeees!' scream the little girls in their
little party dresses as they run towards the stage,
'Yeeeeeeees!'

One chunky young lady in bicycle shorts, cropped
bob and a decided look of Victoria Wood, was pulled

up on stage to be ceremonially straddled, rubbed up against, crooned and moaned over by one of the strapping lads whose programme notes read 'Can you feel the chemistry? Gary has a degree in chemical engineering, but the real Gary has an explosive personality and rock hard body that gives off more heat than a lava flow. He'll keep you safe from wild beasts, but beware – who's going to keep you safe from Gary?' Finally he dropped his boxer shorts and draped them around her head. She sat there, maroon with pleasure, grinning inanely as if he'd draped her with diamonds instead of a pair of sweaty gatkes.

Another woman was lured up on stage for a tête-à-tête romantic dinner. 'Do you wanna be wined and dined by candlelight, girls?' 'Yeeessss! Yeeesss! Yeeesss!' screamed the post-liberation generation, waving their hands over their heads like so many baptists at a revivalist meeting. It's quite the oddest theatre audience you'll ever encounter. They are largely people who've never been *inside* a theatre before. They think it's a pop concert. They come and go when they please, think nothing of walking across in front of the stage mid-number and seem to go to the loo an unjustified number of times – and I have it from one, who has it from one, who has it from one who knows, that the number of garments and objects uncommon left littered about or thrown on the stage is nobody's business, and I'm glad it's not mine.

I was wildly intrigued. I wish I could say I'd been

turned on. We all picked our favourite of course. Mine was kinda bookish and quiet – a bit like Clark Kent before he turns into Superman. Half-way through a number where the lads sashayed on with plastic bottles and sang whilst rubbing themselves *all over* with bronzing oil, I turned to Sandra and whispered hoarsely over the screaming, 'I think I must have some hormones missing. Does this turn you on?' She laughed and rolled her eyes somewhat ambiguously, so I turned to Astrid. 'I was just like this at pop concerts! Like an alien species. What is happening to all these women and why isn't it happening to me?'

At this point speech was taken away from us by the sight of the butchest and most rabid of the lads performing an orgiastic routine with a larger than life banana, which eventually responded to his ministrations by spurting cream all over the stage. I suppose I've seen more horrible sights in my forty-six years, but I'm hard pressed to think where or when.

'Are they as demanding backstage as *I* was in *Re:Joyce*?' I asked Jeremy over an extremely long and extremely cold drink during the interval.

'My dear, the arguments we have over how much Nivea Cream goes in the banana you wouldn't believe!'

Apparently the really serious business is the Polaroid session at the end of the show. Almost every woman in the 1077-seater theatre wants to go home with a picture of her and her chosen Chippendale and she is willing to pay five pounds for the privilege. And to get close of course – she wants to see if it's real or just two pairs of tennis socks and a shuttlecock. Now the boys get to keep the fivers – it's a kind of incentive to make them really work their asses off up there, a bit like Commission Sales in the old Derry & Toms, only this time Derry gives it personally to Tom and Tom sticks it down his G-string and keeps it. Pyramid sales?! Oh God, I'd love to have gone up but I simply didn't have the guts. And it really works. Those guys earn every penny. They never stop. They bump, they grind, they climb up the scenery, they do backflips, they dance, they sing, they wiggle on their bellies like snakes, they flap their flippers and pump their stuff – and if my lad was up there I'd hire a charabanc and take the whole family for a fun night out. His Grandma would be particularly proud. 'No, he was ever so good. He really stood out, didn't he? Mind you, he could do with a haircut.'

Afterwards, clutching my 'Oh my God' sized G-string and my 'Chippendales' Tahitian Adventure' Calendar, we three from Happy Drome tottered out into the balmy night air of the Strand and drove weakly around to the Haymarket to pick up Amy who'd been to see Paul Schofield and Vanessa Redgrave in *Heartbreak House*. Standing there with my Chippendale programme whilst Alan Bates and Helena Bonham Carter and just about anyone who's ever been anyone came blinking out from three-and-a-half hours of George Bernard Shaw, I got the feeling that, on the whole, I'd probably won hands down on style if not on content.

The puzzling bit is this. Have we really gone through generations of feminism from Emmeline and Christabel, through Germaine and Gloria, by-passing equal pay, sexual equality, crèches, reversals and backlashes, in order to achieve the very privileges which are least admirable in our male counterparts, i.e. the right to scream 'Gerremoff' at partially clothed men whom we've never met and are never likely to see again?

PS I've finally got round to *Basic Instinct*. It seems we've also won the right to savagery, cold-blooded murder, nymphomania and total amorality, too. No wonder Germaine's retired to the country to cook her own geese.

Easter-Egg'tomy

'The doctor said I might as well have it done,' said I over meatballs and rice around the family dinner table.

'Have what done?' said the child who'd been listening.

'Fibroids, love,' I replied, ever the up-front parent. 'They're sort of fibrous masses which grow inside the womb.' Amy put down her meatball fastidiously.

'So what do they do to them?'

'They take out the womb – no, it's OK. You don't miss it, honestly.' Her face registered pure disbelief.

'But I don't want them to take away your womb! It was my first home.'

It was a good point. I hadn't actually considered it in the light of getting rid of a house without considering a sitting tenant, as it were. Over the coming months my daughter's comment was to be the least confusing of the ones I received.

'Fabulous,' said a dear actress chum. 'I was up and about and back in a musical in six weeks. It's the best thing I ever did. Honestly – your hair gets better, your skin gets better – you'll feel a different woman!'

'Really?' I disputed, purely on the grounds that I felt happy with the one I was. 'Oh. That's good to hear.'

'Oh I *am* sorry,' said another. 'You must give yourself at least three months of absolute total rest – and I mean you don't even pick up a blender! None of that opening Tesco's on Sunday mornings and saving Dolphins on Monday lunchtime that you go in for ... Absolute rest! Go to the Seychelles for a month with Jack.'

'Really?' said I, closing the bulging diary quietly. 'Oh. Well that's good to hear. I'll call the travel company right away...'

'Oh it's *nothing* these days,' said Mother dismissively. 'Everyone I know's had one. Dorothy had it when she was twenty-nine. Shall I come down and stay while you're in?'

'But why are you doing zis?' said my French amie, Simone. 'I 'ave 'ad fibroids also and my gynaecologist she just took them out and, *voilà*! I went 'ome the same day!'

'Really?' I went. Again. 'Well, that's good to hear.'

'Ring her. At least get a second opinion. 'Ere is the nombre.'

I rang her. The second opinion was crammed in between *Start the Week* and a speech at my old Drama College. It was 'in and out' in most senses of the phrase. Fortunately it confirmed the first opinion. I was, and not for the first time in my life, opinion-sated.

'Just remember,' said a woman I hardly knew, but for every detail about her womb. 'Just remember, you're bound to get weepy afterwards – it's only natural – the hormones will be all over the place. Make sure they give you HRT and take a small pillow in to press against the wound.'

I took a positive stance. This was *not* going to apply to me. I was not going to weep on cue on the fifth day, come over all wobbly on the sixth and demand a refund on the seventh. *Au contraire!*

This was going to be my finest performance. That of a brave woman. If necessary I would be doing the crocodile joke under anaesthetic – and I'd be back on stage in eight weeks if it killed me, as fit as a fiddling flea.

Ten minutes later I found myself weeping incoherently as I dismembered an economy sized box of super Tampons. Pathetic. I mean who in their right minds would miss having periods? Me. That's who. Suddenly that small navy blue box with the unbreakable cellophane cover spelled romance, fecundity, mystery, femininity and *youth*. Maybe I'd just put off the whole thing. Jack could drop me at the hospital – I'd wave goodbye, go in, come out again and head for Heathrow for a longish holiday, just me and my adorable little fibroids. Little! What did I mean little? At my first check up, they were oranges, apparently. Six months later they were grapefruits. If I funked it now, by the time they opened me up there'd be a couple of watermelons, a barrow load of ugli fruits and I'd be shaped like Roseanne Barr.

I thought of that first consultation. My three queries to the gynaecologist had been, 'Look, this won't interfere with my sex life will it?'; 'Had you better just examine my breasts while I'm here?'; and 'Well, can't you just suck 'em out?'

What must he have thought of me? A middle-aged nymphomaniac with an internal fruit stall. No, it was time. I took a positive stance, girded my loins, whilst I still had loins to gird – packed an overnight bag, and went in to get without.

The anaesthetist, bless him, rang me on the Sunday before to promise me I wouldn't:

a) wake up during the goriest bit and be too paralysed to politely point out that I'm in agony, b) never wake up again; or c) lose my immediate memory and keep saying 'who am I?'

Then he said: 'Do you have any crowns on your teeth?' I laughed somewhat mirthlessly.

'Almost exclusively,' I replied. 'In fact if you can find a genuine tooth in this mouth, there's a bottle of Asti Spumanti and a Cadbury's Cream Egg in it for you.'

'Well it might be an idea to ring your dentist and ask him to make you a gumshield because people sometimes crack their crowns by grating their teeth when they come round.'

I could hardly wait to phone the dentist. I could feel the punch-line bubbling to the surface.

'Hello Martyn – It's Maureen Lipman. Sorry this is such short notice. I'm having a hysterectomy on Wednesday – could you possibly make me a gum-shield?'

Putty in his hands really. At least I'll be able to get back into the rugby scrum when I come out of hospital.

Amy was decidedly wobbly chinned when I dropped her at school on the morning of the op. Jack had started treating me like a hundred-year-old Chinese egg. My friends all phoned and made moving little speeches about how they'd be thinking of me and Mother was on the bus from Hull, her fish frying hat in her holdall.

In actual fact, the way I see it, is this. Ten days in a nice hospital room and eight weeks at home with no speeches to make, no grey wigs, no learning, no laundering, no lifting, all the yoghurt balls I can eat and no womb for complaint at all.

The Muddle Classes

I sometimes wonder whether my initials – MDL – were accidental or prophetic, coming as close as they do to Muddle, Meddle and, more pointedly Middle, as in Middle Class. Being middle class is a bit like being a middle child – always slightly afraid one won't fit in, or worse, that perhaps one shouldn't really be there in the first place.

All this spun through my mind in the wee small hours as I was trying to calm my heart down after a particularly clichéd dream at 6 am. I unclenched my jaw which was set in a manner reminiscent of a Remington Microshave and tried to work out why I had removed *all* of my clothes in my friend Lizzy's mother's kitchen in front of *quite* so many people, and donned blue satin shortie pyjamas with a murmured apology of 'Quite close in here isn't it?'

Fear of exposure dream. Classic. Caught on the

loo in front of Her Majesty. 'Doing it' with Andre Agassi in the hardware department in Selfridges' basement. Standing on stage at the Theatre Royal Drury Lane with the curtain about to rise, no idea of the play, the character, or the lines, John Gielgud and Mike Nichols in the Royal box and me, of course, naked. But for flippers and a Band-Aid.

Pardon me for future (Er – allegedly future) Queen-dropping but I was sitting next-but-one to Princess Diana at a 'do' recently wearing all manner of beige linen, discreetly creased and the only hat amongst six hundred women (boy! was I pleased to see the band of the Grenadier Guards! Busbies!), when it struck me that I was feeling at my most middle class. In the sense that HRH could not have been more approachable, charming and generally good fun, the other guests were easy and pleasant and the food was *not* proffered on a silver salver by bewigged lackeys who sniggered when you dropped runner beans on your suede peeptoes. I knew my heart was cardio-funking because I was due to make my speech in fifteen minutes and I knew that my torric lens had spun around forty degrees to the left and the first words of my speech now read 'High Loyal Rowness, Dailies and Mentalgen', but mainly I knew I was suffering from what-the-hell-am-*I*-doing-in-this-hallowed-company-itis.

Old readers will know that whilst others present at the function had with them their wives, their lovers or their personal fitness trainer, I had my mother. Later, after the official line-up, the princess said to me, 'I met your mother. She tells me you drag her along everywhere with you.'

'"Drag her along" is not exactly how I would describe it Ma'am,' I murmured. 'Drag her along' implied some kind of duress. Did you ever *see* the programme about the Siamese twins who were joined at the head? Yes. Well. I'm sure you understand then why a fleeting smile lindy-hopped across my lips and I choked on my designer water.

After my speech it took me about twenty-four hours to come down, and almost a week to stop feeling poorly. Fear of Exposure you see. Will I cock it all up? If not, why not? Middle class. Neither 'nowt nor summat'. I remember driving home from the theatre in a Rolls-Royce recently with a couple of friends and during the journey the owner of the Roller told us that he was hoping to buy a marina. Quick as a flash and with no irony intended, I said 'Why on earth would you want to buy a Marina when you've got a lovely car like *this*?' It brought the car down and no one joined in more than me, but actually I had meant to be interested and polite rather than funny. I wonder how many famous witticisms were witty by accident not design? Dotty Parker was pretty middle class wasn't she? Although, let's be honest, anyone, challenged to include the word 'horticulture' in a proverb, who came up with 'You can lead a whore to culture but you can't make her think' is in a class of her own.

To be honest my problem is less to do with class than with my neurological affliction. The diminishing space between my brain and my mouth. It's alarming. Sometimes I fear that my wit is just begging for the addition of the letter T.

Last summer I attended a high-powered lunch at a historic Pall Mall club, on, it is worth mentioning, the hottest day of the year – you know, the one that signifies three months' solid rain is over and the hose-pipe ban can make its comeback. So there I was, my floral silk sticking relentlessly to prominent bits of me, when the gentleman opposite, who was something equally prominent in the fashion trade, took it upon himself to admire the said dress.

'Super fabric,' he said 'those are all next season's shades, jaunty and bright, as we come out of the recession.'

'I'm delighted to hear it,' I smiled. Then, unnecessarily, 'I've had it for four years. If I hang on to it for another season, will I get to be ahead of my time?'

'I shouldn't really be peering at your dress,' he laughed. 'I should be looking at the lady who's in it.'

'That's OK,' quipped I, 'it's the business you're in.' (I could have stopped there but my mouth was ahead of me.) 'I'm just thrilled you're not a gynaecologist.'

It wasn't the most apposite exchange for a luncheon based around the concept of Judaic–Islamic relations – but with the temperature at ninety-five degrees it certainly broke the ice.

Did somebody once say, 'You can take the girl out of Hull, but you can't take Hull out of the girl', or did I dream it?

Wide-Eyed and
Speechless

There was a time in Ancient Rome when a Christian was about to be thrown to the lions in a vast amphitheatre before the Roman hordes and the Emperor himself.

The lion approached the Christian and circled him, growling. The Christian bent down and whispered in his ear. The lion stopped and skulked away, tail between his legs.

Astonished, the Emperor ordered another lion to be sent into the arena. Again, he approached the Christian and prepared to spring. Again, the Christian whispered in his ear and the beast withdrew and skulked away.

Amazed, the Emperor called the Christian over: 'You are a free man,' he told him. 'But before I release you, you must tell me something – what did you whisper in the lion's ear?'

'Well, sir,' replied the Christian. 'Nothing much really. I just said "I wonder if you would mind saying a few words after you've eaten?"'

I've been doing a bit of speechmaking recently. Raising the old profile for the odd buck for a good cause. It's an effort, it's often time consuming and nerve jangling, but it's never without interest. As Joyce Grenfell once said, 'You learn a lot, most of it good for the work, all of it good for the soul.'

I often begin the speech by saying, 'Don't I look thinner in real life?' It's *true*. I do. Much. It gets a hugely affirmative response and pre-empts them whispering the fact to each other. It also seems to break the ice quite nicely too. (There is a story of the actress sister of Gladys Cooper, who gave up show business because every time she came on stage the audience seemed to be hissing at her. In actual fact, what they were doing was whispering to one another 'She's Gladys Cooper's sister. She's Gladys Cooper's sister . . .')

Basically, my job is to know enough and care enough about the designated charity, to effectively do a balancing act between laughter and pain, and to use one to benefit the other. In other words, I'm there to make the audience laugh so much that their handbags fall open.

The fact that most of the work undertaken so tirelessly by all those committed committees should be part of the business of government is another question. Chicken and egg. If the great-hearted public are prepared to cough up for Telethons, Marathons and Cyclethons, Walkathons, Mountaineerathons and everython bar bonkathons, and I wouldn't put *that* past 'em frankly, then why should the government use their resources for anything other than the Great British Flogoff-athon, leaving us with little faith, no hope and endless charity.

Let's face it, we baby boomers – those of us who overdosed on cod liver oil and Parrish's food and still sport hundreds of metal fillings care of post war goodies, us baby boomers have got to come to terms with the fact that our kids must give up at birth the rights we thought were our birthright.

It's all part of Baroness Thatcher's Major legacy. Come up with the goods yourself or the existing goods will perish. It may hurt the individual, but it's good for society as a whole. Like seal culling I suppose. Oh well, you lot voted them in again, chunter, chunter, mumble, mutter, moan, whinge . . . And look at what she's up to these days – two bubbles short of an Aero!

When I read, recently, in that bastion of faction, the *Sunday Times Magazine*, that my fee for public speaking is £4,500, my mouth fell open and my handbag fell shut. Since I'd never been paid, to my knowledge, so much as a penny for a public speaking engagement, I was intrigued to know a) how they arrived at such a figure; b) who it was being paid *to*; and c) if there was any chance of a few return engagements during the lean season.

Now for the sweet denouement. Since the article appeared, I have had two offers to do what I normally do for gratis at the salary kindly set for me by the *Sunday Times*. Ironic innit? Who says newspapers don't have power? (Actually, should I accept the offers, I will have to skim off a percentage for the person whose lines usually get the biggest laughs of the evening. My very own Golden Girl, Zelma. I merely have to report, truthfully, that Mum is the mistress of the rhetorical question, then, by way of illustration, list a few of her best ones, to get the best of responses: 'Doesn't a black skirt cover a multitude of sins?', 'Aren't eggs useful?' and my favourite, usually when asking directions, 'Are you there?'. Then there's the one in the kitchen, holding up a little piece of black metal, a screw, or a piece of crumpled paper, 'I say, is this *anything*?' And the beauty, loudly whispered during the film *Chariots of Fire*, 'Do you like films about running?'.)

Stories about mothers and children are universal levellers and so are the stories of heartache and suffering and courage which inevitably emerge at charity functions. At a luncheon to save 'The Battered Women's Refuge' in Chiswick, I learned that a huge percentage of batterers are middle-class professional men, dentists, judges and executives, etc. So much for my prejudiced view of a Stanley Kowalski clone reeling home from the pub in a stained, sleeveless vest. The story that hit *me* between the eyes was the woman whose husband

hated her to go out with her friends and always
caused a scene to prevent her doing so. On one
occasion, she had asked him if it was okay for her to
go and he'd repeatedly said yes. She had bathed and
fed the children, left him a lovely meal, checking
again before dressing that he didn't mind. Finally,
she washed, dressed, made-up, said goodbye, checking again that all was well and left the house where,
as she stood outside the door, he poured a bucket of
water all over her from the upstairs window.

Personally, I would still have gone out. Wet and
dripping. This woman had been made to have such
low self-esteem that she considered herself too
worthless to ask for help. From my ivory tower, I had
no idea that battering can be mental as well as
physical and therefore closer, more identifiable to
the little mental cruelties of which we are all guilty.

At the fund raising dinner for 'The Women's
Therapy Centre', I sat next to a charming art dealer,
who had lunched with Ross Perot. Mr Perot, on
learning he was an art dealer, had asked him if he
dealt in any 'hand-painted pictures'. Alongside 'I
wouldn't employ any man who has a beard or wears
tassels on his shoes', you can only thank your
personal God that he never made it to the White
House and then die laughing. Or vice versa. The
dream ticket would have been Perot and Dan
Quayle, who spells potato with an 'e' on the end.
You've heard of parochial. See it personified. Per-
otQuayle. See, I'd never have got to such an appalling pun without the help of that little fund raiser.

So why should I complain when the next batch of can you, will you, would you, could you's come through the door? So, I don't have an item of clothing left that hasn't been signed and sent off, a recipe that hasn't been duplicated, or a childhood memory that hasn't been regurgitated. So everything I wear has got a red ribbon on it for Aids, a gold heart for Variety Club, a green sticker for Macmillan nurses or a blue potty for Tommy? Of course it has, and of course it should, because at the end of the day, as Des Lynam might say, I'm getting more, much more, than I'm giving.

A Little Learning

I've discovered after a mere forty-mumble years a propensity for learning. Having wasted the allocated teaching years in search of the perfect imitation of the people teaching me, I have discovered the latent pupil in me is burning with attentive zeal.

One year it was Flamenco, which I learned for a TV play and took seriously enough to crack open the cellar ceiling with my persistent stamping on the kitchen floor. (During the TV sequences when I was supposed to be inept I found myself struggling against the desire to do it perfectly, and for months after the show was over I became a flamenco groupie, haunting the Tapas houses of Kentish Town in search of Sevillanas.)

A recent foray was into the wonderful world of the auctioneer. Now I'd frequently wielded the gavel at ladies' luncheons, and it was a cinch. 'So, I've got a lovely voucher here for nail extensions at the "Hard as Nails" salon in Finchley Central – and I'm going to start the bidding at twenty. Do I hear twenty-two? Oh, twenty-five from the lady in the fuchsia jumpsuit – I'm sorry, of course it's cerise. Twenty-seven – this is one you can't afford to miss – you'd be a fool to yourself. YES! Thirty pounds, sold to the lady in the emerald green two-piece. Now ladies, don't fight, it's only a bloody nail voucher. Stop tearing each other's clothes! You'll break your nails!'

Little did I realize as I entered the hallowed doors of Sotheby's, that their auctioneers received a rather more formal training. I was to receive a day's training from top auctioneer Peter Simkin. After one hour's training I was ready to be officially pronounced brain dead.

Readers, you have no idea of the complexity of this business. Peter began by saying 'It's fifty per cent showmanship' at which I beamed 'and fifty per cent mathematics', at which I wished to be beamed up. The thing is that you've got your reserve price, and your commissioned bid price and you've got to work out your starting price and your increments on the bases of these bids not arbitrarily, so that you don't end up 'wrong footed' with the bid resting in the audience and not with the house. Got it? Yeah, me too. I took home my sheaves of notes, phoned up the *Financial Times*, who were fronting the charity, and resigned from the job. Kindness itself, they understood my predicament totally and refused to accept my resignation.

Thus it was that I found myself shaking and quaking with the remnants of a bottle of Rescue Remedy in my stomach, in the Imagination Gallery, auctioning off photos and paintings by the great and the near great to roughly one hundred of the most uninterested people I've yet to hector and fawn upon.

Within seconds of going 'on' I increased the show business percentage considerably and reduced the maths one by about 100%. Wrong footed wasn't in it – I was legless. At one point I got so excited at the prospect of *nearly* reaching the reserve price that I threw in my own bid and ended the evening as the owner of a huge panel of engraved glass which I have absolutely no idea what to do with – although I suspect Jack is aching to tell me.

This year's preoccupation, also brought on by a projected TV play, is golf. Now I'm not one of nature's most natural movers. At school my created position on the hockey field was 'left outside' and my idea of an adventure holiday would be removing a fly from my Tequila Sunrise. However, from the first lesson I felt a smile creep across my face and I realized what the advantages might be of becoming the oldest swinger in town.

Of course I was standing fairly still for my lesson, which is always a big plus. If I could learn a sport lying down, it would be even better (suggestions in a plain brown envelope, if you please). Also, I'm totally in love with the one-to-one system of learning. For a start, you never have to fight for the teacher's attention with the kid in the front row with shiny blonde hair, clean plimsolls and a photographic memory. Furthermore, when you only have an hour, and you know the cost of every minute, you tend not to waste them in gazing out the window at the gardener's pectorals or carving 'Elvis is God' on the leg of your friend's desk.

Anyway here I am on lesson one, bending my knees, keeping my eyes on the ball, extending my wrists and, most complex of all, sticking out my bottom in a fair impersonation of Margaret Thatcher showing concern on a disaster walkabout. My teacher, Peter Brown, a man gifted with a perfect swing and the patience of Mother Teresa, keeps replacing ball after ball as I smash 'em wildly and impressively over the green. By the end of half an hour I'm convinced I'm in the presence of genius, my own I mean, and swagger off the course with the jaunty jowliness of Nick Faldo's Fanny – if you take my meaning. And if you don't you've probably formed your own interpretation which is much more fun.

This burgeoning of confidence lasts roughly till lesson three, when for some reason my nicely co-ordinated limbs go into spastic conflict with my number six iron and my eyes start to work independently of one another. In short, I'm bloody useless and moderately bad tempered to boot. It can, as a sport, bring out the very worst in your nature.

Apropos of which:

A rabbi, a priest and a vicar were playing golf. (I'm sorry I sound like Bernard Manning at a welders' convention, I can't help the way my mind meanders.)

Anyway, this set of golfing clerics were stuck at the ninth hole behind four of the slowest players ever to wander over a green. Finally, in desperation, they complained to the steward about the appalling lack of courtesy shown by the players ahead of them.

'Aha,' said the steward meaningfully. 'My dear sirs, what you perhaps do not realise is that the gentlemen ahead of you are all blind.'

'Good gracious! Heavens above,' said the vicar. 'How churlish are we to complain, when faced with such a shining example of the indomitable spirit of mankind!'

'By all the saints, my sentiments exactly,' added the priest. 'How very humbled I feel and what a lesson it is in patience and forbearance.'

'My sentiment exactly, and manifold,' says the rabbi. 'But tell me, why can't they play at night?'

(I only gave the punch line to the rabbi to avoid letters from affronted Protestants and Catholics. I'm used to letters from affronted Jews – I've got drawers full.)

Meanwhile back at tee-hee, I slowly and laboriously practised that most unnatural of acts between consenting adults until I achieved the knees bent, bottom out, glassy-eyed look so adored by golf pros and mothers who are trying to potty train their children. 'Relax,' urges the golf pro. It's not easy to relax when you look like Rumpelstiltskin on Entero-Vioform.

After six lessons and having recovered some of my early promise, I ventured during my summer hols, on to a Cornish golf course. Shock. Horror. My dear, the legs! All that walking! By the third hole I was desperate for one of those little golf-carts to come and scoop me up and drop me on the nearest piece of Axminster. (By the sixth hole which my friend and fellow holidaymaker Lizzy birdied with ease, and our sons bogied or beagled or some such nonsense, I just picked up my ball more or less manually and lurched on to the seventh with my face to the heavens praying to be hit in the rush by a golf ball and carried off for an early bath. By the ninth I not only knew the meaning of the term 'in the rough' I more or less personified it.

By the time the play was due to be filmed I was as the saying goes, 'quietly confident, Brian'! On my first day of filming I narrowly missed death by golf ball, whilst standing beneath a birch tree minding my own business and eating an Eccles cake. I saw Goliath of Gath's dimpled missive hurtling towards me and threw myself athletically in what, thankfully for the other five plays in the series, turned out to be the right direction. My own fault. Rule thirty-eight of the Golfers' Manual. Never take Eccles cakes on to a fairway.

On my second day I stood in four inches of mud

being soaked to the skin by an overhead fire hose, attempting my first shot.

'I did it! I did it!' cries the character, Peggy, 'I got it in the air.' The ball was supposed to travel thirty yards. I gritted my teeth, thought of England and swung like a pendulum do. The ball left the mud-bath, soared into the skies, travelled about 200 feet, skimming the top of a catering bus crammed with ducking extras and landed just north of a Tupper-ware vat of sauce tartare. My confidence grew noisier. I swaggered past the scores of real golfers flanking the clubhouse, protesting, 'No, honestly. It was nothing – really. Just a fluke. No please – what technique? Gracious me . . .' and swept loftily straight into the loo. The gents' loo.

My finest hour was yet to come. Peggy and her husband were to play a game of life and death golf, winner takes all, sort of thing. I was to swing from a bunker and the ball was to land straight in the hole. Obviously the shot would be faked. My golfing double stood by, ready to oblige. It was obvious she would be sorely needed. After ten minutes thwack-ing away in the sand, I couldn't shift it an inch. Patiently the prop men built up a little egg of sand and placed the ball on top. Red faced and mindful of the gathering crowd, I thwacked again. Suddenly there was a concerted gasp and the air was filled with rapturous applause. I clambered out of the bunker. 'What happened? Who did what?' I blinked myop-ically.

Well, gentle reader, disbelieve me if you must, but

the ball had flown out of the bunker, shot past the hole, hit the tracks bearing the camera, reversed direction and bounced straight back into the hole. Incredible. Useless, but incredible. Something to tell my grandchildren. Something to tell Terry Wogan's grandchildren even.

Meanwhile, even as we speak – well, *you* read and I brag – my son is erecting, by dint of a crumpled page of Japanese hieroglyphics, a seven foot practice net complete with chipping pocket, in the erstwhile tailored lawn. Spiked shoes, spelling death to Amtico flooring have appeared in my wardrobe. I am the sly possessor of a perspex visor, a set of Wilson Graphite clubs and a pair of trousers of such appalling loudness as to make Rupert Bear look like 'Something in the City'. A packet of tees has taken up residence in my contact lens bag, and I don't mean Lapsang Souchong. I could be considered a lost causeway.

So, anyway, as I was saying, this priest plays a sneaky round of golf, on a Sunday. St Peter turns to God in Heaven saying 'Tsk, Tsk. Do you see Father Hannegan playing nine holes on a Sunday?'

'I do indeed,' says the Lord, 'and I plan to teach him a lesson!'

The priest tees off. The ball flies one hundred feet in the air where it is swooped upon by an eagle who carries it a further two hundred feet and drops it into the waiting mouth of a rabbit who carries it on to the green, where a mouse kicks it up against the flagpole and a swarm of gnats push it straight down into the hole.

'I thought you said you were going to teach him a lesson?' gasped St Peter.

'That's right,' says the Lord. 'Who's he going to tell?'

I promise it won't last. Honestly. After all, I now use my squash racket to strain fettuccine, my castanets to frighten rooks off the bedding begonias and my unicycle is propping the door open. 'It's just,' as my home help is prone to say, 'a phrase she's going through.'

You just can't get the right staff these days. Come as you were party, 1991.

Ms Streisand: 'Don't look now, your Royal Highness, but isn't that Maureen Lipman's mother behind me?' (*Syndication International*)

Pushkin: 'If those two luvvies would just gerroff that sofa, I could finish shredding it.' (*Colin Poole*)

Post scripts from the hedge. (*Colin Poole*)

Mug shots from *About Face* – and I'm the mug in question.
(*Sally Smith*)

Old Girl's Reunion: Miriam Margolyes, Mary Henry, Libby Morris, Beattie and Toni Palmer. (*Dave May*)

Which one of these women is nearing the end of her BT contract? (*Dave May*)

Laugh? I thought I'd Di. Entertaining the Princess at her
birthday lunch.

All I *said* was 'We got ONE hundred thousand for the King's Head
Theatre!' Anita Dobson, Denis Lawson and Sheila Gish.

A still of Joyce and me from the TV credits of *Re: Joyce* – all credit to the Graphics Department. (*Robert Hill photographer, Linda Sherwood-Page designer*)

'Si Signora. We 'ave it in ze pink and in ze green . . .' Richard Wilson and me renewing our TV partnership in *Carry on Columbus*. (*Island World Productions Ltd*)

'Oh *please* let us join the Garrick Club, Mr Nimmo.' Derek and I in *The Cabinet Minister*. (*Fiona Hanson, Press Association*)

It's Migraine Not Yours

Some kindly but misguided person has sent me a newspaper cutting which claims that scientists are claiming that migraine attacks can be cured by sexual intercourse. I would like to claim that this particular claimant thinks that these particular claims are put about by male scientists seeking to bring down the age-old adage 'Not tonight, darling, I've got a headache.'

Only someone who has never suffered from migraine could make such an obscene suggestion. It's about as apposite as suggesting horse-riding for a slipped disc, or double-sided tape for obesity.

The thinking behind the theory is, I presume, that any relief from tension – i.e., pleasurable feelings, orgasmic release, or hanging upside-down, crowing, from the Tiffany lamp – will relax the muscles which are contracted through the pain.

Ye-ee-es, Mr Scientist sir, your honour most venerated, white-coated dick-brain – but has it occurred to you that once you are in the migrainous condition, it hurts to walk, to bend, to sit, to stand, to *blink* for God's sake? What therefore, is the sufferer to do during this so called love-making? Lie there immobile and thudding whilst their partner does the deed hovering over the bed attempting coitus without interrupting the air, the duvet, the bed springs, or the person beneath.

I mean, I've heard some preposterous proposals in my thirty-odd years of being a head banger, but this latest one takes the Bourbon. The thing is that as with all chronic ailments nobody has the faintest idea what the bloody things are, why we have 'em or what to do when we get 'em. So I suppose suggesting sex is about as sensible as suggesting synchronized swimming.

My mother tells me she had a migraine every Wednesday from the age of about fourteen.

'I used to wake up and think "Ooh it's Wednesday and I haven't got a migraine",' she muses, 'and five minutes later, I'd have one.'

My daughter claims she knows when I'm getting one because I always wear green. This should give a much needed clue, except that half my wardrobe is green and I can't just chuck 'em all because every so often my face matches my clothes.

Jack broke our hearts once by telling us that one of his earlier childhood recollections was of clutching his hair and saying 'I've got a 'neadache'. But a 'neadache is something you and your chosen prescription can cope with. The insidious nature of the migraine beast is to respond to certain medicines until one starts to rely on them, then quite suddenly fail to respond, leaving one with a year's supply of chosen drug, a scudding skull, and a mouth like last year's Bilberry yoghurt.

Talking of food. If I tell you that neither a piece of chocolate, a grain of coffee nor a morsel of cheese has passed my lips for hundreds of years, that I've given up all bread but rye and that the demon alcohol, including red wine and champagne, has been utterly exorcised, then you'll understand that, combined with the old ethnic dietary laws, I'm probably not everybody's ideal dinner guest. Oh and before you start on the old acupuncture and homoeopathic miracle myths – been there, seen 'em, got the Tee-Hee shirt!

After a recent operation I had ten weeks on a prophylactic which apparently opens the blood vessels so wide that constriction cannot take place. It's a little hard-hatted constriction worker if you like. I *hate* being on drugs on a regular basis, but the 3 pints of blood I'd been given had a terrible effect on me. I'm sure the person whose blood I was being fed meant me no harm, may even have been a BT user, but he/she/it had obviously just had a cheese sandwich, a bottle of Château Neuf du Pape, a couple of chocolate mousses (mice?) and a cappuccino. It wasn't very nice really. This is not a plea for sympathy – I'm too angry to need pity. It's blood I'm after! My own! Of course, nobody – but nobody – on the medical scene, believed that my migraine had anything to do with my blood transfusion, in spite of the simultaneousness of their appearance.

'*It doesn't happen*', they told me, to whom it happened. Still, I must be the only woman who had major inuterine surgery and howled 'My head! My head!' every time she saw a doctor. Also, it sure took my mind off my stitches and I'm not unused to going into hospital with an old complaint and coming out with a new one.

Only my acupuncturist Dr Bich believed me. He had seen blood transfusions in Vietnam which drove migrained patients out of their minds. He told me it could go when the blood passed through.

'How long does it take for the body to replenish its own blood supply?' I whinged.

'Oh about 100 days,' he replied breezily.

In front of me is a neurologist's list entitled: 'Precipitating Factors of Migraine Headaches'. It reads:

1. Lack of Food. (Lady Elizabeth Longford, incidentally, has cured her migraines by eating little and often, i.e. every two hours). Pasta is highly recommended. Fasting/missing meals, too little food, snack salad sandwich.
2. Specific Foods: cheese, chocolate, alcohol, red/white wine, Chinese food, coffee, tea, other.
3. Sleep: too much/too little.
4. Hormones: periods – before/during/after; post menopausal/the pill; premenstrual/pregnancy.
5. Head and neck pain: eyes/sinuses/neck; teeth or jaw – a dental gumshield is recommended.
6. Environment:

heat/cold/light/noise/cinema/shopping/parties/smells.
7. Exercise or travel.
8. Allergy.
9. Stress: during/after.
10 Smoking.

Otherwise, it seems, you can more or less do what you like. It's a wonderful life if you don't buckle at the joints. Oh, and for hypermobility – which is if you are double-jointed (yes, I'm that too. I used to be able to skip with my hands clasped together by wriggling through my arms – don't even think about it. This is generally accompanied by thin, loose skin, which gives me something to look forward to, doesn't it?), a soft surgical collar is recommended. Incidentally, while queuing up for my soft collar, the lady next to me, who'd sadly had a mastectomy, asked me cheerily if I would mind signing her prosthesis. I did. So there we are. To stay healthy all I have to do is avoid food, light, entertainment and stress and to sleep in a gumshield and a surgical collar. Sex wasn't mentioned but, let's face it, it didn't need to be. This is a contraceptive which could cure the world's over-population problem in a night!

Meanwhile back in 'Science-land' people with pounding heads and green skin are no doubt lining up to try out the new miracle love-making cure. I wonder if lines of dishy young medical students are forming a queue round the corner to donate their services in the cause of medical research? Hang on, maybe this needs a rethink. Mind you, with my luck I'd undoubtedly find myself in the placebo group and end up getting a migraine every time I have sex!

Column Beau

Last April I received a writing prize. I was voted 'Columnist of the Year' by the Periodical Publishers' Association for my monthly column in *She* magazine. I was very bucked by it but didn't give up the day job – you can see that by the greasepaint in my ears and the ginseng in my bum bag.

It's just that I'm not used to getting prizes. Mostly I just give them. At Functions. With a little bit of witty badinage, a sincere-ish smile and a dress that cost a fortune, doesn't fit and can never be worn again after it's been featured on the telly and in the 'Where are they now?' section of the *Sunday Bollocks*, along with my back molars, a pronounced squint and the words 'Still shopping at Oxfam, Mo?'

The occasion of my scaling of the columnists took place one evening when I was playing *Re:Joyce* at the

Vaudeville Theatre. I got an inkling of this when, a month earlier, *She* editor, Linda Kelsey, phoned my house for a chat with my husband. This is not a common occurrence and could mean one of three things. One, *She* wanted him to write a piece on living with a woman who juggles her life. (It could have had an interesting angle, since I recently purchased, at some expense, three small bean bags and a book entitled *You can Juggle in Ten Easy Lessons* – you can't.) Two, *She* was going to make me redundant and wanted to know what kind of Swatch I'd favour. Three, Ms Kelsey and Mr Rosenthal were having an affair and everyone knew about it except me and Nigel Dempster.

Now Jack is noted for many things, like his glorious prose, his soused herrings and his forbearance with the natives. What he is not noted for is his ability to disguise a secret. Not only is his face an open book, but the back of his head is a luminous poster.

'Er, so ... Er, so ... Are you saying ... er ... (lower voice to *Deep Throat* level) that ... er, she isn't to ... er, (cough, cough) know about this ...?' by which time 'She' has not only pricked up her ears but has pricked up her entire body and had she a prick to prick up she would have pricked up that too, which could have made an interesting column in itself, if you take my meaning.

Suffice to say that he came off the phone, did some studious jotting with his back to me, in order to rearrange his face, failed, and turned to me with the smirk of an eleven-year-old schoolboy who's just traded two conkers for a picture of Gazza weeping in a jacuzzi. Then, concentrating violently on something in the far-left corner of the kitchen, he informed me that I *might* have been shortlisted for the 'Columnist of the Year' but there were *nine* others on the SHORT list (surely an oxymoron, or compiled by one?) and anyway, they weren't *sure* yet but just in *case*, he would be going along with Linda on the night but that was *all* he knew and where the hell have I put the Emmenthal 'cos he hadn't eaten all day and could consume a flock bed if necessary.

Fade out, fade in, and a few more somewhat shifty telephone calls later came the night of the 'do'. Before leaving for the theatre I wished him luck and asked him what he would say if I got the gong. He grinned beatifically and said the three words guaranteed to make a scriptwriter a happy man – 'there's no speeches'.

I picked up a cherry cake for the interval refreshment from a pile of shopping I'd done earlier and acknowledged, with a wave of the said cake, Jack's pantomimed reminder through the study window that he would meet me after the do in my dressing room. I then headed off in search of West End traffic.

I dumped the cherry cake on Sally, my dresser, with a cry of 'Cherry cake for tea!' (I can't over-emphasize the importance of interval refreshments in a show which runs for over two hours with one person doing the running. I have been known to be thinking of nothing but ginger nuts and oatmeal crumble all the way through a spirited rendition of 'I Like Life'.)

Some time later, with the sound of a somewhat underwhelmed audience still ringing in my ears, I was greeted at the dressing room door by Sally in a state of mild amusement, having attempted to slice up the cherry cake I'd given her, which had turned out to be six packets of assorted white cotton-gusseted knickers from Woolies.

At the end of an evening of farinaceous deprivation, I scraped off Joyce's face and headed glumly for the stage door. To my astonishment it opened to reveal my husband in glamorous black tie. Perhaps 'What are *you* doing here?' was not exactly what he expected me to say but it's what I said. Then followed a litany concerned largely with the impossibility of dressing in a dress suit without recourse to a wife. Apparently collars snapped open, bow ties refused to bow, cummerbunds caused instant sciatica, small black shirt studs leap-frogged unaided into the middle distance and links separated themselves from cuffs. It seemed he had changed outfits three times in almost as many minutes. Perhaps 'What are *you* doing here?' was more than ill-advised. He certainly hadn't been picking up the 'Wife of the Year' award! He had, however, he revealed after a bit of abject necking and a Jaffa Cake, picked up the 'Columnist of the Year' award for the wife. Well. You could have brained me with a Teflon skillet. It was only when he told me the competition – everything from *Computer Journal* and the *New Statesman* through to the *Beagle Owner's Bugle* – that I began a crimson flush which lasted a few hours, and was not entirely to do with my time of life.

At the end of the same week, I celebrated my birthday and in the interval received a real iced cake with candles and singing. I also received from my number one son, Adam, a poem, listing every grumble I'd ever grumbled about him and his habits. It ended:

But I could never get frustrated
With one in whom I once gestated.

Mother of the Year? Perhaps not. Listen, a girl has to settle for the award she's awarded.

4

Goodnight Ladies

Re:Joyce Re:Corded

Saturday: 'Last night of last run of *Re:Joyce* at the Vaudeville. Usually this causes me some relief as daytime becomes mere rehearsal for night when in a one-woman show and you are the one woman. This time I'm told the set will be burned and I start weeping at the warm-up.

'Two shows and one glass of warmish Aqua Libra later with advance Sunday papers on lap, mushrooms on toast in digestive tract and finest bath in living memory running down plughole, I know I'll survive.

Sunday: 'Till today. For tonight we *Re:Joyce* for a cancer charity. This entails working from 5–10.30 without food or drink. I beg for sustenance afterwards and eat signing autographs for doctors. Still, tomorrow, and freedom looms.

*

Monday: 'Husband Jack to LA leaving laborious notes for household. "Amy, check driving lessons", "Adam, find your missing trousers. They'll be in some rancid pile at school.", "Maureen, the cat will only eat freshly boiled fish. *Please* be sure to remove from freezer", "Esperanza, please see that dishwasher has salt!". He knows this house cannot function in his absence. He goes. I open tin Whiskas Tuna for cat. She wolfs it. I stand outside son's school looking ferocious till Headmaster takes pity – "I'm waiting for Adam to send him back to look for his trousers." Head looks bemused: "I saw him in Assembly – I'm almost sure he was wearing trousers then." Kids and I eat tenderly hand-cooked dinner together and play cards. Two videos, *Crossing Delancey* (aaah) and, after the kids go up, *9½ Weeks* (aaagh!).

Tuesday: 'I start to scrutinize the house, noticing unmentionable horrors unnoticed during the last ten weeks. Maliciously, I write 'Please clean me in dirt on the bathroom tiles. Dress and don pearls. I'm due at a Westminster Council room to help save the 'King's Head' Theatre Club from sudden death after their grant was halved by London Borough Grant Committee. It's magic. The Tory councillors really *do* sit on the RIGHT and for the most part have blue hair. The Labour councillors really *do* sit on the LEFT and have "abazigly dasal todes" and the Lib Dem really *does* sit in the CENTRE in a woolly beard and macramé sweater. The condemned thespians all do their pieces, flying the flag for the Fringe and, bless 'em all, the capped council coughs up.

'Leaping and kissing like an action replay, we retire to the pub to celebrate. Ambiguous gloom descends on me afterwards in the cab as I realize that on 7 July I'm going to perform *Re:Joyce* in aid of the King's Head to an audience at the Shaftesbury Theatre who've all read that we've got the grant back. I console myself with knowledge that director, Dan Crawford, hasn't had a salary in 16 years. Bless him he just takes the odd pound from the till when he needs a doughnut to see him through.

Wednesday: 'Blank – my Mother invariably had a migraine on a Wednesday. As far as I'm concerned it doesn't exist. If it did, I p'raps had a haircut during it.

Thursday: 'Phone call, mid-morning, from friend Julia McKenzie en route to some fabulous "knock-down prices can't afford to missem 'ave we gone raving mad we're fools to ourselves" clothes warehouse out on the M4. "Get in the car and meet me in Teddington," she orders, and, Pavlovian in my devotion to my wardrobe and my friend, I obey. The North Circular and Hangar Lane are at their most diabolic and I arrive guilt-ridden, moist and cursing. Racks of wonderful designer clothes all make me look like Gertrude Stein in drag. I'm having "one of

those days". Too big for a 12, too small for a 14, face
2,000 years old, hair like a dead rook – and the
minutes ticking away till five o'clock when I'm due
back in Muswell Hill to meet the man from the Wall
Bed company in my son's bedroom. I arrive home at
6.14 and only half-way through a discussion involving recessed shelving and black ash veneer do I
realize where I'm supposed to be. The invitation on
the wall confirms it. Thurs. 7.00.

'I'm supposed to be on the Martini Terrace of
New Zealand House at a reception for supporters of
the Alzheimer's Disease Society. Except that I've
forgotten to go. This is not only seriously funny it is
seriously alarming.

Friday: 'Jack returns from LA to find his wife, at
9.30 am, somewhat haphazardly arrayed in full
evening dress, being oil-painted by a lady with
chains on her spectacles in the upstairs study. I am
unable to greet or kiss him from my stationary
position so he waves forlornly to the canvas. Friday
night, candles and braised organic steak (not on the
same plate) *en famille*, Jack fills us in on "pitching"
a script to a Hollwood exec of at least twelve years of
age and we fill him in on how much genuine grievous
went on in the last *GBH*.

Saturday: 'At 11.00 a lady calls for me to take me to
the Methodist Church for fête opening purposes.
I'm in my braised steak spattered dressing-gown and
have no idea of the charity involved or what area my

speech will cover ... Eleven minutes later I'm on a small stage, "one two threeing" into a microphone and giving it. It seems to go down OK. Dinner at friend's with a girlfriend whom I later drive to a taxi in Park Lane. Home at 1.45 am to find she's back at the party on the phone to comatose Jack, having left her handbag, (i.e. her life) in my car. We call a mini-cab and Jack Sellotapes the handbag into two carrier bags. We nod off. At three she rings again to say it hasn't arrived. This time it takes longer to nod off.

Sunday: 'I'm icing a cake for a friend's birthday. The kitchen and I look like a nursery slope. Girlfriend of last night rings to apologize and to tell us the cab arrived at her home but the bag was so tightly sealed she had to wake her husband to undo it before she could pay the driver. Two o'clock, just the one Hendon Hospital fête to open, in pouring rain with faulty sound system and icing sugar down my bra. Home with bags of herbal massage oil, raffle tickets and dried flower arrangements, I continue icing till 9.30 and cleaning up till midnight. This has been my first week off. "For God's sake Anne," I scream at my agent, "get me a job."'

When the last West End curtain came down on *Re:Joyce* the one woman it came down on was distinctly moist-eyed. Aside from one performance at Chichester later in the year and a quick trip to the Isle of Man to entertain the guests at Lizzy's mother's eightieth birthday, it was the last time I would lurch into 'Lumpy Latimer', sail through 'Stately as a Galleon', or end an evening by whirling into infinity: 'as weightless as an astronaut, all fluidity, rising up and over the surface of the room, the street, the countryside. I need no music. I am the music, and the movement.'

It was a tough, tender parting. More like leaving home, or college or a perfect marriage than coming to the end of a long run in a play.

'Don't you miss not doing the play, Mod?' Amy would ask me after every other West End run.

'Nope.'

'Oh, you must do. *I* do. I hate not being able to come in with you on a Saturday. And don't you miss Sally (my dresser)? And Derek (my hairdresser)? And the *songs* – you *must* miss the songs?'

'Nope. Not once it's over. No really. I mean it. I'm just so happy to stay home at night, and, well now – I don't know how I did it. I can't remember a word of anything I've ever been in.'

'Well, *I* can.' She can too. Words, music, movement, relative qualities of the other actors. If ever there was a small critic in the making, this is she.

But *Re:Joyce* is different. It doesn't really fade. It's part of me. I just have to dust it off and spray it and it's fresh as a Marguerite and twice as durable. And virtually audience-proof. A lot of time and discussion went into 'which theatre' before we settled on first the Fortune and then the Vaudeville, but in my heart of hearts I knew it didn't matter if we did it in the Express Dairy with two chairs, one piano and a couple of hats from the Sue Ryder shop. I've performed it in a fifteen foot living room in Connecticut to an audience of eight and at The Maltings at Snape to two thousand. It went fine on both occasions. Arrogant of me? Don't think so. It's not me. It's Joyce and me.

Recently I visited Brookfield School in Highgate to encourage the reading programme by sharing my favourite books and poems with kids aged from five to twelve. It was one of the toughest audiences I've faced. Once they'd clocked that I wasn't old and fat with a receiver clamped to my perm ... they were fairly ready for an early milk and biscuits, or whatever they give kids these days, Aqua Libra and gluten-free rice cakes I suppose. Still, I soldiered on, through Ogden Nash and Jean de Brunhoff and 'The Seven-toed Cat' and 'The Mouse Who Played the Balalaika' with my inimitable imitation of a many-stringed instrument using soft palette and lower molars. Then I made the fatal mistake of asking their opinion, and the whole place turned into *Blue Murder at St Trinian's*. Accordingly, acting purely out of instinct, I clapped my hands together and launched into Joyce's nursery school sketch ... 'Children, children, now gather round because today we are going to do our lovely moving to music. And Miss Boulting is going to play her piano and we're all going to be *lovely* flowers, growing and dancing in the grass. *Isn't* that nice? Yes it is Sidney...'

There was a silence you could've cut with a Swiss

Army spoon, punctuated only by burst of delighted 'allowed' laughter and when I got to, 'Oh Lavinia, what do we do when we get back from the littlest room? We pull our knickers *up* again', they took the roof off! And they say that nothing dates like comedy. It's not entirely true. Fine, relevant, truthful comedy – aka the best of Chaplin and the Marx Brothers, and, I believe, Joyce Grenfell – is perennial, one just needs a couple of decades away from it to re-appreciate it thoroughly.

When I flew over to the Isle of Man to do *Re:Joyce* for Madge's eightieth birthday party, I had the problem of having to use an accompanist from the Isle of Man. Madge told me the name of the hotel pianist who would be playing for the dancing. It was Mark Stevens. He would be pleased to accompany me if I sent over the music. Subsequently, I mailed over the sheet music for four songs, along with a cryptic commentary on the lines of: 'Dear Mr Stevens, thank you so much for agreeing to play for me. I shall do just the first and last verse of "I'm Going to See You Today" and it should be in the key of F; "I like Life" will be one verse and a chorus only and in the key as printed. "Stately as a Galleon" is in the key of D and I will not be singing the second verse. The cues are as follows, blah, blah, blah and I look forward to seeing you on the 12th. Yours, etc. etc.' Not knowing his address, I mailed it to the hotel and asked them to forward it.

When I arrived on the island, Lizzy picked me up at the airport and drove me to the Castletown Hotel.

After checking in, I asked the receptionist whether Mr Stevens had received my letter.

'Yes, I'm sure we gave it to him. You can ask him yourself – he's over there in the armchair. He's staying in the hotel.' She gestured to the foyer where Mr Stevens was sitting reading a newspaper. I approached him.

'Mr Stevens? I'm Maureen Lipman. I hope you got my lett ...', the words died on my lips as I realized I was talking to a very elderly man indeed. If this gentleman was my pianist, then he probably learned his trade in about 1910. I swallowed and tried to continue: 'Er, my letter, did you ...?'

He rose, unbending his frail, elegant form from the wing chair and took my hand. 'Oh, yes, Miss Lipman, yes indeed I did.' He smiled the sweetest smile. 'Quite a surprise actually.'

'Oh, yes,' I stammered 'Erm, did you find it terribly confusing? I'm sorry I shouldn't have sent such a scrawl ... can you make it out?'

His smiled broadened. He was very slight, immaculately dressed and, in his youth, probably very like one of those fashionably askew young men who pop up in the ravages of Waugh. What worried me at that moment was whether a full rehearsal and two hours at the piano would do what two World Wars had failed to do, and see him off.

'So, do you see any immediate problems?'

'Well, no. I'd be delighted to help you, dear lady, in any way I can. But you see, I don't play a note.'

Pause. 'Pardon?'

'Er. The piano. Don't play a note. Never got the hang of it.'

'I see. Oh dear.' My mouth felt like brushed denim. The scenario swam past my lenses. 'Come Into the Garden, Maud' accompanied on the euphonium. 'So what exactly is your instrument?'

'Well, er ...' He chuckled. 'I was a bit of a dab hand at the spoons in my youth – that's about the best I can do.'

Pause. I sat down, my mind racing. This was going to be some musical extravaganza. 'I don't understand. They told me you were the hotel pianist. You *are* Mr Stevens, aren't you?'

'Yes, indeed, but ...'

'Mark Stevens?'

'No. Owen Stevens, and I'm absolutely delighted to meet you.' He looked at my look, 'and if I can possibly help you in any other way I most certainly will.'

It was fine. No really it was. So, I lost a few years off my life span. It was nothing that a couple of weeks at Grayshott, a couple of needles in my left ear and a heart transplant couldn't cure. I found the real Mr Stevens, the one who *could* read music. The one who could read music and played it on, wait for it, the electronic synthesizer! Oh, Joyce, what would you have made of it? We arranged to meet later and I went over to Madge's beautiful house, full of my adventure, to find the bogus Mr Stevens sitting sedately on her sofa. He was an old and dear friend and had flown over that day from Chichester for the celebrations.

The evening went exceptionally well, give or take a few unusual high pitched sounds from my radio mike, warring with the real Mr Stevens' synth. It was a perfect party and the following day I flew home from Manx's tiny airport where the lady in the Manx Kipper shop told me I put her in mind of that Maureen Lipman, only younger. Later that year, Owen came to the Chichester Festival Theatre for another rendition of *Re:Joyce*, this time with a real piano. He brought me a lace handkerchief and a book of his wonderfully silly puns and poetry called *Random Ramblings*. He was in the most charming and innocent way, I think, a ladies' man. He sadly died this year, before I had a chance to tell him how much I enjoyed reading them – they were full of music.

The televising of *Re:Joyce* was a co-production by Prime Time TV, an independent company, and BBC2. You might have thought that a show which had sold out three times in the West End, required only two salaries, one piano, one simple set and for which the costumes only needed a rub down with two mothballs and a pils-remover, would have been easy to sell to a TV company. You would have been wrong. My agent, Anne Hutton (who was also Joyce's agent), Robin Lowe, her literary counterpart and I tried every television company with the offer of a ready-made show and, to a manager, they turned us down flat.

The Independent television franchise auction was

in the air, very few programmes were being made at all and those that were had to be of potential mass interest and, presumably, look seductive on a brochure.

BBC2 had run Joyce's own, late 1970s TV shows the previous Christmas and the viewing figures were in the millions, which proved her lasting appeal but also may have discouraged the ITV companies from showing interest in what they saw as a humble copy. Central TV pricked up its aerials for a few minutes, then withdrew contact. Even the BBC showed no interest at all when first approached by the very experienced recently retired director Yvonne Littlewood, who has staged most BBC spectaculars up to and including the Queen Mother's ninetieth birthday gala, and was very interested in ours. Shortly before the last West End run from March to June 1991, we approached Richard Price of Prime Time TV and a meeting 'was taken'. Richard, a veteran of televised comedy, the prime mover behind the sales of the 'Brit-com' to American TV and that year's BAFTA Chairman, felt that he could budget *Re:Joyce* for one week's rehearsal and two evening recordings in front of a live, studio audience. There was a strong feeling that the show could work equally well if it was recorded live in the theatre in which we were appearing but I was equally strongly against this. However sophisticated today's cameras are at picking out close-ups from fixed positions, however precisely the show can be edited afterwards to cut out the 'heightened' acting, the projection one uses to perform to 700 theatre-goers will always make the show look like a hybrid: half theatre, half television and wholly unreal.

The invited studio audience, so beloved of sit-coms and Robert Kilroy Silk, was the best compromise. It gave me something to time the sketches around. It gave us the approbation and applause which we'd come to love and to need. All we needed now was the 'co' in co-production.

I left it in Richard's capable mitts and took one of the Rosenthal familial holidays in France, so lovingly chronicled in a later chapter. I was stuffing shoes with socks and spreading dry-cleaning bags over unnecessary woollies, when a phone call from Richard told me we were on. From a black hole of uninterest into a virtual skirmish between BBC2 and Channel 4, the BBC had emerged victorious. I was almost moved to shout "Yo! BEEB" and throw the odd flip-flop in the air.

'Thank you Joyce,' I muttered slightly more than *sotto voce*. Marmaduke Hussey, the Chairman of the BBC, is the husband of Lady Susan Hussey, Joyce's and Reggie's niece. I like to think his aunt-in-law had a spiritual word in his shell-like. Why not? If the mountain won't come to Mo . . . Ham it! The bad news was the script was one hundred and thirty minutes long. For the purposes of the BBC slot it needed to be one hundred minutes only. I threw out the Ambre Solaire High Protection Factor, shifted three lurid paperbacks and packed the *Re:Joyce* script, a large pair of scissors and some tape.

Under azure skies in a large hat and shades, I circumcised my baby. Only then did I truly understand Jack's agony when a TV play is found to be twenty minutes too long due to 'directorial flair', and whole scenes, whole sequences, whole storylines – all of which work beautifully – have to be cut to save time. In fact, it's only since I started writing myself, in any capacity, that I recognize and marvel at his patience, his forbearance and his ability to pick himself up, dust himself down and start the whole bloody, silly business all over again. Out went old favourites, in came tenuous links and sometimes I just abandoned all pretence and wrote 'leave this in for now. I'll say it *dead* fast I promise.' Amy typed up my scrawl each night in the hotel bedroom on her 'Little Brother' computer. Her real little brother lay comatose in front of CNN reports. During the second week, the creative team from the BT commercials flew in, bearing Tricosa gowns and Beattie's grey wig. They took over a suite, measured me up for new padding, tried thirteen outfits on me, talked 'bottom-lines' by the pool of the Hotel Cap Ferrat and flew out, leaving behind a couple of tricel scarves and a distinct whiff of expense account opulence. As a holiday it was, to say the least, an unusual way to relax from the vigours of a year in show business.

On our return, I went straight into rehearsals with director John Reardon re: *Re:Joyce*. John had directed me in three series of *Agony* between 1979 and 1981 and we were old chums. He and his lovely spirited wife, April, endearingly referred to by John as 'Grunthuttock', had seen and loved the show on stage, and he was steeped in the kind of knowledge for which a mere three weeks' pre-preparation time could hardly have prepared him. Stage director Alan Strachan, was around to keep my mind focused on the 'why' and not the 'how', and Geraldine Stephenson, choreographer, Denis King, my accompanist, Sally my dresser and I all fell upon each other like immigrants in a new but familiar country.

The technical run, when the TV crew arrive on the day before the recording, was hair-raising as usual. Dozens of strangers pile into your sacred rehearsal room. They pore over folded plans and camera scripts in tight knots of like-folk, sound huddled on one side of the room, lighting on the other. The rehearsal starts and they don't look up. Then, gradually, as though listening to a background radio comedy, one of them gives you the merciful gift of a snigger and encouraged, or just by osmosis, a few others join in, until just before the interval, some intrepid technician, probably the designer's assistant, looks up. Then just when you think you've got him, tea is announced, and you all retreat back into your peer groups. The difference in the second half is in the knowledge that if you've got one, you can get *all* the buggers and that you'll never play a tougher house. The final laughter and even, yes, applause, is the most sincere you'll ever encounter. In spite of themselves, their floor plans, their innate shyness and the pill of invisibility they took before they came in, they've enjoyed your turn.

This technical run for sound, lighting and cameras in the studio on Friday, in costume, started at 10.00 am and finished at 10.00 pm. When you're 'on' constantly, you don't, as it were, get off, so by 9.40 pm I was ready for an early bath. Afterwards in the canteen over dusty Danish and BBC tea, Shawn Sutton, the charming avuncular veteran of just about every good BBC drama ever made, told us stories from his own particular archives. They were marvellous. He ended with the apocryphal story of the young boy who goes to a lady of the night (his expression) for his first sexual experience. He's very timid, but she does her best to make him feel 'at home' and everything goes according to the oldest plan of all. Half-way through, however, when he's really in full throttle, she leaps up in the air and he falls to the floor perplexed. 'What's wrong? What did I do wrong?' he gasps.

'Oh, I'm ever so sorry, duckie,' she replies, 'it's just that I heard a door slam and I thought you'd gone without paying.'

On Saturday we continued the technical run until 5.30 pm when I went into make-up, and at 7.30 the invited audience were 'warmed up' by Bobby Bragg and the show, as shows must, went on. I felt subdued but fawning loved ones assured me it was fine. Denis was nerve-less as he had been throughout the techs. 'It should be called *Re:Denis*,' I grumbled.

The next day's recording, Sunday, was to be a safety valve, so we could pick up any bits of the show which didn't work the previous night. That was the idea anyway. In actuality, the audience was a third empty because of some ludicrous overbooking and dear Denis Norden, introducing the show as a very personal favour to me, had to defrost a very cold house. I was infinitely better but Den said he felt awful. On the whole, though, it was a better show. But could we use it since the quality of laughter is much less by definition with a three-quarter full house? Afterwards, Prime Time gave us a drink and a nut or two and they, and the BBC representatives, seemed pleased but then, how the hell can you tell whether an executive is pleased or not? Does he loosen his tie? Smile with his eyes? Scratch his left ear? Who can tell? It's like the joke: *Question:* How can you tell if a politician is lying or not? *Answer:* If he touches his nose, he's telling the truth. If he smooths back his hair, he's telling the truth. If he adjusts his collar, he's telling the truth. But, if he opens his mouth . . .!

The show was lovingly and laboriously edited by John Reardon and John Sillitto and went out prominently on BBC2 on Christmas Eve, looking much better than I'd ever imagined it could with so little time and such a small budget. All credit to John and the producers.

Joyce's husband, Reggie, and his immediate circle were all delighted, and the hundreds of letters proved what we'd always known – that there is a huge audience of people out there who are largely neglected and uncatered for. They want to be amused and entertained without being patronized or having their intelligence insulted and, if possible, they'd like it to be musical. I think my most sublime moment came with a handwritten letter from Sir John Gielgud, who knew Joyce well, saying stuff that I immediately memorized but am too coy to tell you. It almost made up for the blow in February when the first BAFTA TV list came to the house for Jack's member vote. This list, the first round 'long list' usually contains everything that any member can nominate from *Blue Peter* to *One Man and his Dog*. Everything, that is, save *Re:Joyce*. It didn't even make the long list. Outraged, I rang Prime Time's office to find that it wasn't on the list for a very good reason. Nobody had nominated it. The BBC left it to Prime Time to do it. Prime Time left it to the BBC. Producer Shawn Sutton wasn't a member. Richard Price of Prime Time, who was also the Chairman of BAFTA, had been out of the country. My husband hadn't thought it was necessary because he was sure the producer would do it. And I wasn't a member. It was something of a disappointment, particularly so, since the Olivier committee had done practically the same thing with the stage show. Their defence was that *Re:Joyce* could not be considered for an award because there was no suitable category into which it could fit. It wasn't a musical, it wasn't a play. It was an 'Entertainment' and in the wake of their dilemma, a new category was created. The following year.

So every time I read, and I read it a lot, that

Maureen Lipman and Denis King will be perform-ing their 'award-winning' show *Re:Joyce*, a papery smile flits across my lips and I have to be very firm about thinking how lucky I am that the kids are healthy.

Pressganged

The bell finally tolled on the BT ads after its privatization campaign. I think we made eleven commercials in a couple of weeks and employed every Jewish actor who had not previously appeared in them and several who were as Catholic as a Kennedy but just came along for the ride. It was a riot. When Miriam Margolyes, Libby Morris, Mary Henry, Toni Palmer and I were in the same room it sounded like Babel. Except we all spoke the same tongue.

The first time I shot any BT ads, we had the great hurricane. I drove from Muswell Hill to Wandsworth, through three desecrated parks. It felt like the end of civilization. Bearing in mind that we only shot for two weeks, twice a year, it was odd that we were shooting through the Gulf War the time before last and the Russian Coup this time. Believe me, this is not the last vestiges of my own megalomania – 'My part in World Crisis by Beattie' – it's just that, frankly, it kept things in proportion when often they felt grossly distorted. I rarely keep a diary but a few scrappy pages from 19 August read:

Monday: 'Up at 6.00 am for 7.00 am car to Studios. Sally and Tracy (wardrobe) in car. Into costume and make-up by 9.00 am. Still sitting in dressing-room at 12.30 – nothing filmed. Richard Phillips is directing but hasn't written these scripts ... this one features Reece Dinsdale as privatization telephonist. Nice actor. Richard and I quietly doctor script. Grubby (producer) asks for two working Sundays extra, twelve commercials as opposed to eleven, one personal appearance in November, and newspaper advertising and poster featuring Beattie. We skirt round problems and agree to one and two but not three and four.

'Home by 7.00 pm for Jack's salmon salad tea, delicious. Amy is painting friend Amy in oils. I work on Joyce script, talked to Prime Time TV financier, Nigel Whitehouse, Denis, Dan Crawford of the King's Head and crash out at 11.30. 'P.S. Imagine! I didn't mention the coup in Russia, Gorbachev on holiday. Hardliners take over. Yeltsin in Parliament building. Sounds very serious. Something tells me it won't work.

Tuesday: 'Studio by 7.00 am. Migraine hovering.

Richard on super-waffle, has Adrienne Posta
and Lionel Haft giving me "off-lines" in a
small room, off the set, all day. Down a
phone. Mom arrives by bus from Hull to
Golders Green. Amy goes to Wiltshire,
Adam to friend Will. We don't start filming
'til 12.00, so I have plenty of time to phone
home. No words can describe the indescrib-
able. Melvyn explains privatization to Beattie. Long protracted gag with Harry and
newspaper won't work. We never finish the
shot. Day is hot, tedious and endless, take
after take after sodding take.

'Adam made evening meal. Took him
three and a half hours. Hors d'oeuvres,
chicken and salad, lychees and jelly. Washed
up and did errands. Something has been put
in his drink during his stay at Will's, obviously. Russian tanks advancing on Moscow.
Yeltsin holding out. Fear the worst. Shots of
rioting crowds in Red Square. Troops fire
gunshots. I'll never complain again.

Wednesday: 'Better day. Left home 7.45 am, chatted
to Miriam Margolyes and Bernard Bresslaw.
We endlessly repeat the scenes. "Melvyn,
guess what? I'm with Dolly and she says . . ."
then, "Melvyn, I'm with Dolly. About these
BT shares . . .' then fast version, then slow
version, then very fast, then very slow. All
day on one scene. Home for eight o'clock for
Mom's chopmeat. Letters to write, phone

calls to return. Jennifer (dresser from America) says she'll come over to help in house while I'm on tour (Esperanza having announced she was going to Colombia for two months). Tanks turning back. Leaders of coup fleeing in badly organized limos. Yeltsin talks to Major. Gorbachev to Bush. It's over. History live in the making. Feels like the last gasp of communism.

Thursday: 'Decent morning. In bed with Harry in bedroom. Very hot set. Padding, flannelette nightie, wig, etc. Script – "It was awful. I dreamed it was the 6th December. I hadn't phoned my cousin, Ettie, to remind her it was the last day she could get her BT shares." Then, same only "I dreamed it was the 5th December" then "the 4th". I kept fluffing it. Got it finally but after we did it millions of different ways. More and more takes. Lights are burning down. Studio full of people. Harry has no lines. All responsibility on me. John Reardon, Shawn Sutton and Nigel Whitehouse came to the set for lunch to discuss *Re:Joyce* TV. All gob-smacked. After years in TV can't believe the time wastage and general faffing about and number of different permutations and re-shoots for no reason. "How do you *stand* it?" I smile and concentrate on Russia. No money for *Re:Joyce*. Budget of £170,000 for whole show. Same as budget for *one* commercial.

'Afternoon, back on set, back into bed. This time they've changed lines to "It was awful. I dreamed they'd closed the BT shares offer and I haven't phoned my cousin, Ettie, to remind her", plus some new pillow thumping business. The copy writer's name seems to be Charity Charity. We do it thirty or forty times. Suddenly Richard wants one more take. I weep. Weeping becomes wailing and keening. Thinking of Russia no help. Hunched and pathetic I lurch out of bed moaning. "I. Am a human being." (Just like in *The Elephant Man*!) "I can't work. Like this. (Gulp.) I don't know what's going on – what sentence to start on – what version –" I head for the door. Alex, liaison secretary for McMillan Hughes the production company, runs after me. "I'm so sorry – I'm so sorry." Helplessly, dripping and gulping for breath I get in the shower, tidy up, start to feel guilty. Richard says he's sorry – I say no, it's me. They send me home.

'For some reason my mother finds the whole thing hilarious because I'm wearing red-and-white striped top and shorts – she's helpless with laughter. Jack and kids comfort me. I say "It's five o'clock now – in about fourteen minutes the flowers will arrive." Nine minutes later the doorbell rings and Adam collapses with laughter as he brings in the bouquet. It's the cliché to end 'em all.

Say it with flowers. Say *what* with ruddy flowers? "I'm sorry I can't decide what I want until you've shown me every possible permutation of what I *don't* want – so can we get on with it or we're *all* in the shit?"

Friday: 'Much better day. Calmer – not so many takes – jollier atmosphere. We did three short commercials with nary a cross word. Better out than in, clearly.

Saturday: 'Roots done in Berwick Street. Stall-holders all friendly "'Ello Maureen owery-adoin'? Ya gorra great cheese shop in Muswell 'ill – keep it up gel, we love ya." Over to Denis's for rehearsal, for tomorrow we *Re:Joyce* in Chichester to 1300 people for one night only. I'm terrified I'll forget it all. Haven't done it since April.

Sunday: 'Drive to Chichester. Very scared. Thrust stage theatre and three sides. Scamper through show to empty house and clattering stagehands. Rest in dressing-room. Show is a delight. They interrupt sketches to applaud. "Hello" songs are received uproariously – and from then on in we can't go wrong. Den goes very mid-Atlantic in middle of First Act and I drop a few lines in "Countess of Cotely" but end of Act I applause is heavenly. Second Act quieter response but Mrs Moss, (the terrible worrier, who wins a rabbit in a raffle and doesn't want it) gets great response and hysteria from someone

on my right which nearly makes *me* go up.
End of show you could hear feather drop. We
exit to thunderous applause, kissing the air
like Dietrich.

27 Aug, Tuesday: 'Back to work. One whole commercial filmed starring Sonia Fraser and
Calman Glass. It was a lovely day. Never
thought I'd say that on a BT shoot. Richard
in marvellous mood – cheery and explana-
tory – and we all behave beautifully. Sonia
Fraser exceptionally good – an interesting
women – she directed Miriam Margoyles'
one-woman show *Dicken's Women*.

Wednesday: 'Same again with Libby, Miriam, Mary
Henry and Toni Palmer. My God. The
noise. And the people! Great day, for them
'as like a laugh.

Thursday: 'Barbara Young and I in identical dresses
as two wedding guests in a stifling studio
marquee. Barbara is an old friend and her
daughter, Cory, aside from being a gifted
actress and singer, is one hell of a good
masseuse. With her own table, noch!
Richard Phillips is wearing bermudas and a
shirt with "Dick" embroidered on it. I
become silly with tiredness and say to him as
he stands frozen in a trancelike state of
thought – "Can I touch your 'Dick'?" He, of
course, has forgotten he's wearing the shirt
and his face was perfection!

Friday: 'Migraine in night. Nurofen in morning.

They are filming street scene with old friend
Stella Tanner and Barry Martin in a posh
car. Geoff and I at the bus stop. Alex, bless
her, has organized location four minutes
from my doorstep – I'm slobberingly grate-
ful. Conversation between Stella and me,
waiting for shooting, is classic. We are discussing someone, who shall be nameless
[unless you write to me enclosing a stamped,
addressed envelope and a mint humbug].
"He was such a shit", "He sponged off her",
"He always put her down", "He really upset
my husband", "Well, *nobody* liked him. . . ."
etc., etc.

'Barry Martin, standing by earwigging,
said "Who are you talking about?"

'Me: "Oh, just a friend."

'Finished ad by 2.30 after a location
lunch. Amy and Mum came by. Sat in
garden 'til sun went down. Two videos and
proper kip.

Sunday: 'Blinding migraine in night. Drugs at 4.00
am. Ah, me. Work. I arrive at location in
Archway Road for eight o'clock start. Gifted
and funny actress, Caroline Quentin, playing my daughter, and four year old Kate
plays hers. We are in a taxi cab, supposedly
coming from Heathrow. The taxi cab is in a
low-loader [backless lorry which transports
a car so that it appears, on camera, that the
car is moving]. A camera was attached to the

cab and huge arc lamps blazed down on us from both sides. Instructions came through a walkie-talkie on the seat beside me. On a busy, red-route dual carriageway, it was unlikely that things would go according to plan and they didn't. Consequently, after half-an-hour, Kate, delightfully contained for a four year old, was bored, hot and "Wanna get out now!" was the order of the day. To entertain her I removed one of the "prop" holiday gifts from its packaging. It turned out to be a small, black, charging bull with "Present from Malaga" pinned to his hoof.

'"Hello, little girl" said I, in a growling sort of voice and a defined and somewhat perverse Michael Horden-esque accent. "What are you doing here? More to the point what am *I* doing here?" Kate's already enormous eyes widened about a foot and she solemnly took up the conversation, as only an intelligent four year old can.

'"Well, you see, Mr Bull, I'm doing this advert and Maureen is being my grandma and we're in this taxi pretending to go home. Are you hungry, Mr Bull?"

'Caroline and I exchanged looks. We were, without a doubt, in for the duration.

'"Yes, I am. I've travelled a very long way in this box, all the way from Spain, little girl, and I've eaten all my straw . . ."

'"Oh, poor Mr Bull, would you like some cake?" She turned to me and appealed. "Can we get him something from the café lorry where my mummy was? Can you make them stop, he's hungry. Don't worry, Mr Bull, Maureen will get you some nice . . ."

'"Oh, no, little girl, that's quite alright, thank you, I, er, I can wait until the scene is over, I mean until we get home – er –"

'"But . . ."

'"Now why don't you tell me your name and who is your best friend?"

'Four hours later, Kate was as bright as a boutonnière and twice as animated. Caroline was slumped in a heap and Mr Bull and I were on automatic co-pilot. It was all we could do to keep the wretched toy out of the scenes. Every time "action" was called Maureen had to say "Mr Bull can't talk for a minute now," then Kate would tell him, then Beattie would say "So, Elaine. Thank God. You're just back in time to register for BT shares," and so on. It was multiple personality and then some. When we finally got out of the cab, Caroline and I had the glazed look of most of the cast of the Starship Enterprise.'

The last Sunday was the last ever shot. It was filmed at the City Airport in the centre of London's Docklands. Beautifully structured, expensively finished, highly polished, empty, arid and anachronistic. A metaphor of Eighties greed.

The scene, where Harry and Beattie meet Elaine and family in from their Spanish sojourn, was shot quickly and with no undue fuss, as the first one had been, some fifty-four commercials earlier. We all said our final, final goodbyes, real affection, flowers and photos were exchanged and that was that. We hung up – but kept our connections open. This week Beattie's remaining wardrobe went to 'Fashion Acts', and Aids related charity, and will be paraded down the aisles alongside the Jean Muirs and the Vivienne Westwoods. A tribute to polypropylene, Crimplene, Terylene and every other 'ene but Maur.

I knew that the privatization campaign was a risk. I knew it could be regarded as politically incorrect to condone privatization when most of my sympathies lie to the left of centre. I knew as well that few actors actually represent or stand up for the product they are selling, that Sharon Maughan doesn't have flagons of Gold Blend in her kitchen and Tom Conti doesn't drive a Vauxhall. The punters who harass me in Tesco's because their telephone bills have gone up are, I'm afraid, twice removed from reality, and probably write letters to Sharon and Tracy's old men in the nick, informing them what their birds get up to each feathered week. Doing an ad is an acting job, like any other. Even if the Labour Party had come into power it was dubious whether they would reverse any of the existing privatizations. So, after forty-four commercials in the can, I decided the die was cast, so was I, and a few more would make little difference. Of course, the moment you try to explain, you sound a) defensive and b) guilty. 'So don't explain' (author's wise husband).

The long term results of my Beattification are still reverberating. Almost without exception every review of everything I've done since, including the second *About Face* series and *The Cabinet Minister* read as follows: 'Making the connection with Maureen', 'More to Maureen than TV Beattie', 'The Beattification of Maureen' and 'Beattie is a real Beauty'.

In the wake of Beattie, the question I'm constantly asked is did I, do I fear type-casting? To say no would be a lie. To say yes would not be the entire truth. What I fear is being accused of taking certain parts in order to *avoid* type-casting. Parts I've actually been playing for twenty-five years. When I've played Shaw or Shakespeare, it didn't occur to any reviewers to write 'Jewish actress tries her hand at Shakespeare' or 'Maureen's Yiddishe Momma is so Shaw footed'.

When a character captures the public consciousness it seems that that character is the only angle that any interviewer wants to explore. This in turn makes the actor pull back. He or she wants to talk about the *current* job, not the last one. Sensing repression, the journalist becomes more Rottweiler-like in his attack and the resulting copy reads like a protracted whine by someone who will do *anything*, including selling their mother-in-law to white slavery, their children to a set of Satanic abusers and their body to Dr Howard Jacobs' sperm clinic, to avoid ever again playing the part which made them a household word. The resulting copy goes: 'Why, I'll never play Beattie/Alf Garnett/Black Adder/Elsie Tanner/Angie again.' This, coupled with speculation of the 'quarter of a million pounds every time she dials' variety puts the nail in the coffin. The final scores are always Tabloids: 10; Actor: Nil. Every time.

Now, it's all over bar the pouting and I can return to being an ordinary satisfied customer. I'll be shorter on perks but may have a longer extension. Furthermore, I need never again receive abusive letters from affronted BT users, such as the one from Christine Keeler, no less, demanding that I stop making commercials for BT whom, she claimed, made immoral profits. Hmmm.

Even furthermore, if I want a quiet moan of my own about the changes in the phone system, I can make them without feeling personally liable.

Sometimes, in my nightmares, I'm endlessly making phone calls. Sometimes I make endless phone calls and it's a nightmare. I realize that I'm biting the fee they hand me, but *I'm* a consumer too, and I too can get consumed.

Take this scenario:

'Ring Ring Ring Ring Ring Ring. You are connected to 190, Telemessages and International Telegrams. If you wish to use this service, please hold the line'.

(Thinks) Well, chutney. If I didn't want to use this service why would I be sitting here being irritated by a pre-recorded telemessage?

Cue: One tinny version of the *Spring* symphony from Vivaldi's *Four Seasons* relentlessly played whether you like it or not. Music while you wait. (Of course, if the machine hadn't been answered until someone could take my call – I probably wouldn't have been paying decent dosh to hear a tune which didn't exactly bring up the crocuses in my nature.)

During the oboe section, a voice says: 'Hello, what service did you require?'

'I'd like to send an international telegram to . . .'

'May I have your telephone number please?' I give it. 'Thank you and could I have the subscriber's name and address please?' I spell both with infinite care, always mindful of the old family story of my much-loved maternal grandfather. He had a deep distrust and fear of telephones. He was a little hard of hearing and picked it up only when it was absolutely necessary. His son, with whom he lived, had an office equipment business and one day someone rang his home to leave a message that the metal chairs had arrived. He was anxious to be off the phone and back in front of *The Good Old Days* from the Leeds Palace of Variety.

'Alright then,' said Grandpa. 'I'll tell him. The little chairs have arrived.'

'Er – no – er – not the little chairs, the metal chairs . . .'

'Yes – I've written it – the little chairs.'

'No – I'm sorry – er, I'll spell it, shall I?'

'If you like then.'

'Right. Can you tell him: the metal – that's M for Mary . . .'

'Right M for Mary.'

'E for Ethel . . .'

'Right. E for Ethel.'

'T for Tommy . . .'

'Er, hang on,' said Grandpa. 'T for what?'

The conversation became well-night folklore in Hull and still raises a laugh thirty-five years after it happened.

Even in those days, Hull had its own private phone company with such divine amenities as a party line (a phone line shared by one or more houses to split the bills). If you picked up the phone and heard a conversation, you politely put it back again 'til they'd finished. By gum, that must have pipped a few clandestines in the bud. I don't suppose party lines exist now. 'Geroff the effing phone, you effing pillock!' would be the order of the day – which takes me back to:

'Yes, the address is Mr Simon Jones c/o The Broadhurst Theatre, West . . .'

'Could I have the subscriber's number please?'

'I just gave it to . . .'

'Yes, I'm afraid I have to ask again for official reasons.'

My sigh is of the variety used by the three old Yiddishe men sitting on a park bench when one, on a descending scale, goes: 'Ay, ay, ay, ay, ay, ay, ay . . .'

into infinity. Then the second goes: Aaaay, aaaay, aaaay, aaaay . . .' similarly. And the third ones says: 'I thought we'd agreed not to talk about the children!'

I give her the sigh. And the number. Again. Then I carefully spell out the name and address of the recipient. 'Mr Simon Jones. The Broadhurst Theatre, West 44th Street, NY, NY.'

'Thank you,' she purrs, 'and the zip code?'

Thinks. The zip code. The bloody zip code! How in hell's dentures . . 'I'm afraid I don't know the zip code but I'm sure . . .'

'I'm afraid the American Postal Service will not accept a telegram unless it is clearly zip coded.'

'Don't you have a book of (sharp intake of breath here) *zip codes* for New York?'

'No, but if you ring 153, the operator will give it to you. Thank you. Goodb . . .'

'Er *Excuse me* . . . excuse me. If I then come back to you with the bl. . . . with the *zip code* (memo: get blood pressure checked in chemist at next visit), will I have to go through all this again or can I ask for you?'

'Hold the line please whilst I check with my supervisor.'

'DON'T GO! Helloooo, *Hellooooooo* . . .'

'Hello?'

'Oh, hello, if you check with your supervisor – will you leave me with Vivaldi and his sodding *season* or can I have the static and the odd pip like in the old days?'

'I'm sorry, madam, but this is the signal when a customer is on hold and I'm afraid I don't make the rules . . .'

'Thank you. I'm aware of that. By all means ask the supervisor . . .'

Da da dadadada da da da ♪ Da da dadadada da da da! There is a small trampoline in my study. Holding the portable phone and muttering expletives, I jump up and down in time to the '*Spring*' symphony.

It is arranged. By giving my name and a few details, I will avoid having to go once more through the whole rigmarole of . . . giving my name and a few details. I suggest a coded message, such as 'My trampoline is gay', but it falls on stony headphones.

I make a cup of tea, eat a packet of M&S Sour Cream and Spring Onion Crisps and dial 153. A pre-recorded voice tells me I have dialled 153 and am waiting in line and in the meantime: 'da da da dadadada da da ♪ da dadadada da da'. I put a finger in each ear, stick out my tongue and make very loud ambulance siren noises. Daa daaa. Da daaa. Da daaa.

'Er, hello? Caller?' It is clear she has been listening to me for some time. 'Can I . . . help you?'

I clear my throat and explain my predicament, ending with 'So can you give me the zip code for the Broadhurst Theatre, West 44th Street?'

'Well, actually, no I can't,' she replies brightly. 'I'm afraid we're not allowed to give addresses, only phone numbers.'

I place the side of my head which doesn't have a phone on it against the desk blotter. It soaks up my tears.

'Tell you what I could do,' she continues, oblivious. 'I could give you the phone number of the nearest post office to the theatre and *they* could give you the zip code!' Zip code. Zip code. The words have become absurd in my brain.

I decide to tell her the mermaid joke: 'What are the measurements of a mermaid,' I say.

'Pardon?' she replies.

'Thirty-six, twenty-four and eighty pence a pound.' I replace my receiver.

'No worst, there is none. Pitched past pitch of grief/More pangs will, schooled at forepangs, wilder (w)ring.' Gerard Manley Hopkins prophetically, poetically on 'the telephone'.

I phone back to 190. And tell another lady my story. She is sympathetic, I'll give her that. She suggests that we could: a) send the telegram without a zip code (in which case, she confides, they'll send it straight back); b) send it with a warranty (in which case if it gets there I pay for it, if it doesn't, I don't); c) send it by phone (whereby it would be telephoned to Mr Jones and written down only if he requested it).

OK. It does not take a member of Mensa or even a member of the One O'clock Club to realize that: d) I could ring him myself, without help from 190 or 153 and say 'Hi Simon. Good luck on your opening with Joan Collins, love Maureen and Jack.' I did none of these things. I wrote this. And now I'm happy. I've bitten through the skin on the insides of my cheeks and I'm all rung out. But it's me I answered to.

Once, many quarterlies ago, when Jack still lived in Blackpool with his parents, he phoned them from a weekend trip to London. His dad, mistrustful of the telephone, always spoke into the ear-piece.

'Hello Dad. It's Jack.'

'He's not here. He's in London.'

'No, Dad, I'm Jack. I'll be back tomorrow.'

'Not yet, he'll be back tomorrow.'

'Dad, you're speaking into the ear-piece. Turn it round. It's me. Jack.'

'Right you are then. I'll tell him you rang. T'ra.'

Consummate communication. It's comforting to know it's still around today.

oBTuary *Beatrice Bellman (1989–92) An Appreciation*

Ladies and Gentleman. We are gathered here today, to mourn the passing and celebrate the life of Mrs Beattie Bellman, duenna of the dialling digit, matriarchal megastar, wife, mother, shopaholic, doting grandparent, *doppelgänger* and, above all, the woman who put the telly into telephoning and tellyphobia on to the telly.

Four years ago Beattie was just a glint in Richard Phillips' Ray Bans. Since then she has captured the hearts and the imaginations of a generation of subscribers, sent their bills soaring and put a smile on their faces even as they signed their cheques. She has turned the reaction to the words BT from an 'Ugh' to an 'Aah'. She has coined the only word in the English dictionary to begin with an apostrophe; she has won twenty-two trophies for her creators (that's more than Gazza and Dame Judi Dench put together); she has inspired a virtual Brazilian Rain forest of newspaper cuttings ranging from the adoring through to the speculative and even a couple of truthful ones; and she has, above all and against all competition, continued to make us laugh out loud.

But as Beattie would have been the first to say 'Every dog has his day', adding characteristically, 'personally I wouldn't have one in the house. Have you ever tried to get dog hairs off Dralon?'

And let us be honest, the new techn'ology, the end of the monopoly and above all the new logo on the vans might well have been a strain on her thinning brain cells. In fact it was in reporting the *price* of the new logo to her friend Dolly on the handheld that she died – in mid gasp. As her husband Harry said, 'She died as she lived – on the phone. Little did I know when I married her what the words "With this *ring*" were going to mean.'

Theirs was a golden partnership – as friends said today, 'a marriage made in Hendon.' Fifty years of total accord and compatibility. Beattie said what she was compatible with and Harry acted accordingly. His strength and forbearance acted as a rock to her gregarious cocktail of barely suppressed paranoia and outright megalomania.

Harry is being comforted in the bosom of his family and his agent is on a life support machine. Harry has issued a statement to say there is no truth whatsoever in the Fleet Street rumour that he has already joined a computer dating bureau in Stanmore, and blames it on the fact that he just happened to have been photographed in *New Man*, buying a silk bomber jacket.

Their children, Melvyn and Bernice, both spoke emotionally of their dynamic mother's sudden demise and the full story of their life with Beattie will be revealed in the *Sunday Sport* under the heading 'Sir Iain Vallance Took Our Mother's Ear' – starting as soon as their residuals end.

Her burial will be quiet, is the family plot – sorry *in* the family plot (please no flowers, just phonecards) – along with twenty-two awards of assorted grotesque shapes and sizes, a grey wig, recently coiffed, a yard and a half of foam padding and the latest BT walkabout module.

The headstone will read 'Now it's *Him* she answers to' and 'Rest in Pip-Pip-Peace. BT: 1989–1992. At last they called in the receivers.'

Finally, a word from her sponsor. Whatever I may have said, not said, refused to say, meant to have said or been misquoted as saying, over the last four years, the commercials are something with which I'm proud to have been associated, and the eighty billion pounds a minute which the press have so accurately reported to be my salary will be missed only slightly more than she will.

5

Anglo File

The Cornish Green

Half a pound of flour and lard
Makes a lovely clacker
Just enough for you and me
Cor Brother Janner

Oh how happy us'll be
Whan us gets to the West Country
Where the oggies grow on trees
Cor Brother Janner

Cos we're all going back to Oggyland
To Oggy-land, to Oggy-land
Yes we're all going back to Oggyland
Where they can't tell sugar from tissue
    paper, tissue paper marmalade and
    jam. Oy!

This, I'll have you know, was the song, replete with Cornish accent, into which my husband, a mature, seasoned and often erudite man, who just happened to have spent his National Service years in a barracks in Devonport, happened to burst into on our first day in Cornwall. The location, The Quaintways Café, Millbrook, Cornwall, the time just approaching mid-day, the effect – shattering. More of that anon.

The facts are that for the first time since our honeymoon, spent in fashionable down-town Bognor Regis, the Rosenthal/Lipmans have holidayed at home in England, and I can tell you that it was a treat. For years we have lugged our luggage across the five corners of the sun-scorched earth in search of exactly what's on offer just west of Plymouth.

Like clotted cream, the Rosenthals do not travel well. The mere sight of a Eurocheque depresses me, and that's without the planning, packing and passport panic. It takes me several days to get into a mood half decent enough to fully appreciate the termites, the unfriendly natives and the half-built villa.

This time, by common consent and a few conversations with Country Holidays Ltd, we just loaded up the boot with the obligatory golf clubs (my fifteen year old son and I have had fourteen lessons between us and are zealots to the course), a cool box filled with stuff we found we could buy 500 yards from the country house, and considerably more clothes than we'd need for a three months' stay at Balmoral. And off we tootled.

It's not a short journey, and the ministry of transport, bless 'em, do like to keep their road-workers nice and busy in the hot holiday months, but the A30 was hospitable and the village of Millbrook was calling us, with the promise of a dammed lake, in the geographical sense of the word, and a house deliriously labelled Lake View.

It was perfect. We all leapt from the car like the Famous Five do when they hit Kirrin Island. Rolling lawns down to the lake's edge – alright the lake was just mud flats on arrival but late that night it filled up something lovely and the boats bobbed beatifically in the setting sun. A Lebanese cedar tree laid its delicate hands on the croquet lawn in front of the house and in back, as the Yanks have it, a small swimming pool winked and beckoned from the terraced garden. The kids marched through the house crying 'Look at the lovely dining table! Have you seen the sloping roofs in the bedrooms?' and 'We've got all our own crockery!' It was a bit like the first time Annie got to visit Daddy Warbucks, but we had to agree that Lake View was just charming.

We surprised Diana, a local lady, putting the finishing touches to the house in the wake of a family from Aberdeen, and I expressed some amazement at the slide out, under-drawer fridge. I asked incred-ulously, 'How do they manage without a freezer? I mean for ice and stuff in this weather?' She smiled and informed me there wasn't much call for that sort of thing down here – but in a manner not calculated to make me feel like an evacuated Londoner, and omitted, kindly, to tell me that it was *her* house we were commandeering and her fridge I was insulting. Within a couple of days, her husband, Peter, had installed a new freezer, which made me feel so guilty that I stocked it up with three months' supply of frozen peas and ice.

From Day One, Millbrook-on-Lake was a triumph. There were seven of us, including Lizzy and her two children, and when we could prise ourselves out of the pool, away from the croquet lawn and out of the village supermarket, we would head off in search of tennis courts and cream teas in nearby Looe. Driving down the steep road into the seaside harbour town, the sun baked down in a most un-English manner. We rounded one last, mildly congested, corner and there it was. Collective breaths were drawn in and 'ooohs' and 'aaahs' gasped out. The old bridge spanning East and West Looe was the clasp of a necklace strung with pearly boats on a shimmery band of blue. Houses climbed the steep slopes on either side of the river. Semitropical vegetation tumbled luxuriantly between the terraces of the tranquil valley. It was Portofino, Monte Carlo, Tropez – with oggies!

I should tell you in case you're oggnorant of these things that an oggy is a Cornish pastie, and my husband decided early on that no day was a good day until he'd had his oggy. We dined at one of the best restaurants I've ever visited, The Well House in St Keyne, where each course was more mouthwatering than the first, culminating in a summer pudding which made you long for a one season year; but nothing was quite as good to Jack as that hot, mid-morning oggy from the Spar bakery.

Which leads me back to our sing-song. When we first walked into the Quaintways Café, it was very quiet. A couple of regulars were reading their papers as Jean brewed up in the kitchen. 'Hello, Tom, you're late today' being the tenor of the chat. Quiet, peaceful and unhurried, it was a bit like a scene from *Straw Dogs*. Until my husband revealed his past by bursting into his song. Auditioning, if you like. As he reached his peak, hoarsely rendering 'Oh brother Janner' Jean broke in 'Oh, noo!' she said. 'It's not "Oh, *brother* Janner", it's "Oh *bugger* Janner"!'

'It isn't.'

'Is.'

'Isn't.'

'Is.'

He patently couldn't believe that 200 foul-mouthed sailors could possibly have bellowed 'brother' when they could have been bellowing 'bugger'. The whole restaurant took sides, and afterwards Jean taught us 'Oi know where the blackbird be', which we've sung on every car journey since. Suffice to say, the café took the Rosenthals to its heart and Rosenthal hearts fell deeply in love with the café.

Next door, 'Mad Mac's Chicken Shack' sold us their original loon pants. It was strange to see almost an entire Cornish village population sporting batique and tie-dye sarongs. Edgecombe Park and its magnificent stately home gave us the scandal of the new (as in New Zealand) Lord of the Manor, the delicious house and grounds at Antony allowed us to roam around marvelling till way after curtains drawn and kick-out-the-tourists time. And the unspoilt twin villages of Kingsand/Cawsand welcomed us in the evenings for food and scrumpy. God's Own Country they call it. Need you ask why?

There are scores of theme parks, barbecue cruises, animal sanctuaries and leisure farms – none of which I can vouch for because I never saw them. We played golf once, I was shocked at the amount of walking involved and collapsed exhausted on Hole 3 of the panoramic cliffside course at Whitsand Bay. The rest of the time we lazed around the pool, read our Peter Ackroyds, ate too much, drank just enough and laughed inordinately at stuff we now can't recall. It was .. well, it was, unlike most fortnights that begin and end with Gatwick or Heathrow, a *real* Holiday.

South of D'Abord . . . er

'The South of France? In August? You must be barking mad!' said Stanley our neighbour and Francophile over the over marinated olives in our local Muswell Hill Deli. 'That's when the French are on holiday – it's Blackpool with Baguettes!' I struggled with an olive pit and swallowed a smile.

'Well, you know, it's the only time the kids can – well, and me – for once I'm not working . . . and besides, I want them to speak some French for G.C.S . . .' I petered out and moved away towards the Haagen Daaz – but both the olive pit and Stanley's smirk refused to move on.

'Whereabouts, anyway?' He persisted.

'Oh it's a place called St Aygulf,' he looked blank. 'It's near St Raphaël,' He looked disbelieving. 'And . . . Fréjus,' he looked despairing . . . obviously I was going on holiday to the Crewe of the Côte d'Azur.

I could have cancelled. But maybe Stanley was un snob. Maybe they only stayed at Jean les Pins on juin le quinze. After all, the Holiday Villas people had told me this villa was a favourite of many of their 'TV people'.

The owners had waxed lyrical about the view and we had rearranged our flights enough times to make me tremble to dial their area code. So we went. Not just for the normal two weeks either. Oh no. The last of the big spenders. We decided that since the villa was empty for a week before we arrived we would, for the first time since weaning, have a three week vacation and *really* unwind! Yeah? And if you believe that, then Madonna's taken a vow of celibacy and I'm a crocus.

The flights were just fine – I unclenched at the English Channel and glanced down at the Inflight book for long enough to note that the other Chanel, No 5, had gone up about twenty-five quid since I last bought any, and suddenly I was looking at the luncheon meat landscape of northern France. Within seconds it had changed dramatically to Alps then quite suddenly your eyes were closed by the luminous blue of the Mediterranean, and before you could say 'Jack Delors' we were at Nice airport trying to separate two metal trolleys which appeared to be copulating – ah well, this *is* France – and into our sturdy little Renault we popped. *Allons!*

It took three entire round trips of the airport before we finally clocked that 'péage' was the word for toll as opposed to the word for a small French town which we did not want to visit.

After that, the journey was punctuated only by cries of 'merde' from the navigator who quickly realized that the directions given to us by the Villa Company hàd been compiled by a computer with a silicone chip on its shoulder. The one hour journey took three. It was hot and Fréjus was fun the first time we circumvented it, silly the second and downright irritating the third. As we neared St Raphaël my heart – which had begun to sink a little earlier – plummeted. The camp sites were spilling out their happy third degree scorch victims. The beach was alive, squirming with bodies lying calf to calf and toe to toe. The sea was one giant red and white armband. And lo and behold, *la pièce de résistance*, there on the jetty's edge was the seaside entertainment: five fully-sized all singing, all dancing, all *Mutant* teenage Ninja sodding Turtles! I retreated further into my shell.

We found the villa. It took twenty-five minutes to master the door locks and get in. Once in, we wished we were out. It was OK I suppose – a sort of cross between some digs I once had in Stratford and the Tandoori Paradise in Barnet. We couldn't find any sheets. The tiny concreted pool was filled with leaves. And wasps. And other stuff we couldn't put a name to. I put the kettle on to cheer myself up. It began to rain. The kids began to fight. I phoned my mother. Always a bad sign.

We spent the next few days trying to decide where to move to. Advice came thick and fast. The Belle

Rives Hotel in Juan les Pins, the Hotel du Cap in Antibes, La Reserve in Beaulieu, La Maas D'Artigny in St Paul de Vence . . . Everyone we knew had something or other to say about where we should have booked if we'd only consulted them first.

Finally, anguished and homesick, we drove along the scenic red-rocked coast road towards La Napoule, just outside Cannes and booked into the first hotel that would have us. The Royal Casino, formerly Loew's, faceless, bland and absolute heaven to the disillusioned holidaymaker. Our intention was to stay there for a few days then move to La Reserve, but once we'd packed and unpacked again we knew that only an invitation from Gerard Depardieu would entice us to do it again. (This in spite of my mother having described him, after a viewing of *Green Card* as having 'a nose like a bum'.)

During the comparative sanity of the following two weeks we sunbathed (our son in his T-shirt 'cos he's well up on this ozone layer business), swam (my husband learning to do so, for the first time in his life, including two years' National Service in the Navy), and constantly and incessantly fed our faces. Le Bistro du Port in the tiny harbour at La Napoule served up their loup de mer and the kind of salade niçoise which reminds you why those particular ingredients were first assembled, and in the pleasant shade of a thirteenth-century monastery, we watched the matelot-striped world go by.

Our neck muscles, formerly as relaxed as Saddam Hussein's right-hand man, began to soften. Adam hit the 'Ski Nautique' and his adolescent lethargy evaporated in a frenzy of enthusiasm to stay upright on a couple of plastic planks. His sister sketched and scribbled wearing a large hat, every inch the Victorian lady with the *Baedeker*. I was lured, with several other barking masochists, on to a water sausage: a long, red inflatable with useless gripping handles which is dragged along at speed through the harbour by a speedboat. The boatman's tedium is relieved only by the sight of flying Englishwomen hitting the polluted bay like discarded grass cuttings. When he's got an empty sausage his cup runneth over.

The evenings, however, were velvety, and Jack and I got so bold that we actually took a stately turn or two around the hotel dance floor. This was beginning to feel almost like a holiday.

Cannes by night was a lively cosmopolitan serendipity of content over style. To my relief it wasn't overtly smart (I can hear Stanley's voice saying – 'Well what do you expect in August? Anybody *remotely* smart will be in Toulouse.'), which suited me and my wardrobe just fine.

Outside the Carlton Hotel we watched the watchers watching for Jack Nicholson and we dined 'al fresco' at Chez Felix, at the next table to the table next to Peter Ustinov. By the harbour some curious jousting men in gondolas tried to knock each other into the river and at our table in 'Le Mal Cassis' arrived some nice English/American villa owners whose daughter had apparently married the son of the sister-in-law of my father's brother-in-law in

Hull. *Petit monde n'est-ce-pas?*

Apart from one day spent relieving myself of an obscene amount of money in a boutique in St Paul de Vence, we scarcely travelled. The medieval walled village had a resonant charm which even ant-like brigades of tourists couldn't conceal. I kept thinking of Bethlehem with its 'Ninth station of the Cross Pizzaria' and hearing a voice saying 'Somewhere in there is a beautiful peaceful town. With inhabitants and a history.' It sounded suspiciously like Stanley's voice.

Lunch at Les Belles Rives in Juan les Pins (Blackpool *without* baguettes) was one of our most lingering memories. It's a coolly elegant, Thirties hotel with real, not illusory, grandeur, and my paella, under striped awnings au bord de la Mediterranean was perfect.

Afterwards the kids and I swam out to a moored raft where I had every ounce of breath in my body removed by the sight of a fast moving, single black fin coming towards us. It was, of course, a swimmer in a mono-flipper. *I* was, of course, a basket case who had to be helped back to shore.

The next day, our last at the Royal Casino, was enlivened by the arrival of a diminutive Sultan in several double limousines. He, in his hybrid cross-dress of Armani crumpled linen and muslin kaftan, ensconced himself in the casino and was no trouble at all. His nineteen bodyguards, however, kept a higher profile, skulking meaningfully about the pool area, pacing the lobby and occasionally freeze-framing by the automatic doors to change their expressions from bored to menacing. We headed out for Moujins to do the galleries and shops, much to the disgust of Adam who had wanted to stay by the pool and perfect the Xavier Perez de Cuellar impersonation he had just discovered he could do in his bedroom mirror.

We accepted an invitation to visit the relatives of relatives and spent a splendid afternoon by their gorgeous pool. The most abiding memory I have is that their loo had a mirrored door. Once ensconced inside with a copy of *Paris Match*, I looked up in horror to realize that I could see through the mirror straight into the lounge, where the entire family had lined up in front of me to point and giggle. Nightmare – this was my nightmare – fear of ultimate exposure. I blushed to the roots of my soul.

As a final treat we sipped Margueritas on the cool, brown-shuttered terrace of La Maas D'Artigny, outside St Paul de Vence, against a backdrop of violet flowered walls and oleander and geranium framed gardens. 'Stanley would approve of this,' I told Jack.

The next day we drove uneventfully to Nice, accepted the plane delay with a sanguinity born of a relaxed state of mind and nicely bronzed souls, and flew back to the most beautiful, elegant, clematis and morning glory covered house in the world. Ours.

Swiss Roll Call

It's almost seventeen years since I was last hauled up a mountainside with a metal bar across my bum, two poles in one hand and my arm around the anorak of an unknown Austrian whose only English was 'Bend ze knees' and 'Open ze legs'. Seventeen blissfully ignorant 'sno-plough' free years with nary a thought of green sunbloc, purple reflective goggles or navy blue knockers and not a knot in my stomach, in anticipation of hurtling off a glacier with sweat running down my long johns into my boot-bindings.

Listen, you know, you've been there, you with your own triangular boots bag and Rissognor skis. You probably go with a gang of friends to the same chalet every February. You have progressed from nursery slopes to post-graduate slopes, struck up a personal and possibly a carnal relationship with Walter (with a V) and can make your own raclette.

Your ski pass probably says 'Life Member' for God's sake.

Not so I. Nope. I'm a natural. A natural beginner. And never more so than on a week's holiday in Switzerland. We had planned, after the rigours of playing eight shows a week for six months, to hit the Caribbean, but I sort of forgot to book. I got a brochure and said 'Ooh look love, poolside cottages, palm trees, coconuts, calypso . . .' and he said 'Sun rash' and that was that really. Then Julia McKenzie and Gerry phoned and they'd booked a chalet near Gruyère with a swimming pool and a sauna and I said: 'Ooh yes – skiing and walking and mountains and clean air' and he said 'Cheese' and smiled, and we were on.

Only Gerry really intended to ski, a fact which was emphasized by an extra piece of luggage which was eight inches wide and six foot long and had a specially designed rack on the car roof. 'Here go the English on holiday', I mused, as we drove from Geneva airport in search of an unmarked motorway, 'four people and two skis'.

The scenery, it goes without saying, is a triumph of mind over Matterhorn. If they had had only one towering, snow-tipped mountain – or just a few – 'twould have sufficed. Enough to make a girl gasp and say 'Stone me'. But to have them all around, everywhere you look, to see frozen waterfalls defrost and move like a slow frame film, to gaze down into valleys, dotted, as it says in the brochures, with carved wooden chalets with roofs like lyres – to have all this and chocolate too, is almost obscene. No wonder they keep themselves to themselves. They don't need the rest of us. (They've got their fall-out shelters under moulded hills, their massive neutral army, their secret vaults and numbered bank accounts – what do they want with the European butter market and 'our men in the Gulf' and Albanian refugees hanging from boats?) They've got more important things on their minds. Like quartz clocks and embroidered hankies and aluminium fondue sets and whether the neighbours are taking baths too late at night.

Oh, and where were the cows and goats? Where were they? Not one animal did we see all week, or hear for that matter, although the small windowed barns on the mountain paths, the frequent smell of liquid manure and the amount of cheese melting on the menus indicated that there must, somewhere, be some. Certainly the snow was on the turn after an unusually mild spell and the chalet in Moléson, which must look picturesque as all getout under a blanket of *neige*, looked decidedly Pontins decked in half-grass and half-ice. (The chalet itself was more of a base camp than one had perhaps hoped for but, fortunately, we are veterans of disappointing villas and chalets and still have the vestiges of a sense of humour in such circumstances.)

'Never mind – it's – it's *fine*. Oh look, there *is* linen. Oh look at this sweet little picture of a cow ... Heavens, they've left a bag of oranges. Oh here's the opener – for God's sake let's have a Campari!' Thus it was that both the sun and our faces were shining when we took the Telecabin up to the top of the nearest mountain and developed a habit which was to stick like gluvein. Rösti. A Swiss potato cake, fried, with two eggs on top. It slides crisply into the mouth and settles snugly in the thigh section of the ski-pants. This became our daily opiate – where to get the best one, whether to have it *en haut* or *en bas* and, ultimately, whether the Telecabin, which took us waveringly up, would manage the infinitely heavier journey down. Lovely though. What could be lovelier? Feeding your face 'neath dazzling sun, whilst perfectly normal people with a death-wish float overhead in striped paragliders or hot air balloons.

And so it came to pass that on the third day we journeyed to Gstaad and ski'd. Not Jack, of course. He's got his head screwed on right. And his right hip as it happens. So Gerry went into a big boys' class and Julia and I went into the kindergarten and stood knock-ski'd whilst infants of three and a half hurtled round poles and flew effortlessly past us down hill. Our instructor was a disaster. (He'd been teaching klutzes like us for thirty-four years and was as bored as the face on a fish. His instructions were mumbled at no one in particular and in no known language.) Bellowing 'Vatch me!' he took off to show how it was done then stood chatting at the bottom whilst we failed to do it.

'My friend has never ski'd before,' I panted, after picking her up out of a picket fence. 'She doesn't know how to stop.'

'Yes, yes, she must not vurry . . . relax. Vait, I show . . .' and off he went again. Showing us. After a triumphant journey of thirty odd feet, unfortunately executed backwards, Julia propelled herself neatly into the nearest restaurant and ordered an early rösti.

I, however, plodded on in the dolts group and once he'd got us up by lift where the air is rarefied, he did the only decent thing a ski instructor can do. He disappeared. For an hour. His party of eight stood around grumbling and scuffing their skis. Except me. Determined to catch up, I did several snow plough turns round a tree, trudging back up, sideways, each time, until my thighs gave way under me and I sat down, leading to the biggest problem I'd faced so far. Getting up. It took twenty minutes, four helpers and, finally, a sort of Kama Sutra repositioning and the removal of one ski. As I stood up, exhausted, Walter returned and began wearily barking out his inaudible orders to turn, to shift weight, to slurry one ski. We followed lamblike, dropping like ninepins at each turn. It was war. One more fall later I began to unfasten my skis in the face of his bellowing. I'd had it.

'Put ze ski back on.'

'*You* put the bloody ski back on mate! I'm walking!' I threw down my fibreglass extensions and made as polished an exit off right as possible, given that my huge orange plastic boots were not made for walking and the terrain was as friendly as blue eyes in Harlem. It took me an hour and a half to walk down a slope which could be ski'd down in three minutes. (Later that century – er – day, Julia and I went to the ski school to complain. The person who took our complaint was so impossibly handsome that the lacerating attack froze on our Lypsyl and we more or less bowed our way out grovelling.)

It will be at least another seventeen years before I go up a mountain for anything other than rösti or a yodel.

On our final day we were entering the Restaurant de la Tour when we heard the cow. It was very close. We ran across the road to see it but the area remained a cow-free zone. The 'Moo-ooo-oo', however, was as loud as ever. We finally tracked it down to a small covered trailer behind a parked car. It was from the inside that the dolorous sound was coming. A cow on its way to its own funeral. 'Oh God,' said Julia as we crossed back to the restaurant. 'Don't anybody have steak for lunch.'

'Noo-ooo-oo!' said the cow under wraps. 'Noo-ooo-oo'. She sounded as piste-off as I was.

There's a Small Hotel

'According to *Esquire* magazine,' confided hotelier Tony Porter in the comfortably faded glamour of his Burgh Island cocktail bar, 'this is the best place in Europe to "do it".'

'Keep your voice down,' I hissed in a manner reminiscent of Del-Boy, 'I'm here for the sea air and the scones.' My husband studied his instep with rapt attention. Well the way I see it is, you can get quite enough of that sort of thing at home.

What you can't get at home, certainly not at my home though I can't speak for yours, is the sheer romance of being marooned, twice daily by a visibly inching tide on a blob of Evening Primrose-covered rock twenty-six acres wide with nothing on it but a white deco liner of a hotel, a fourteenth-century pub, a Ruer's ruin and a barman with a double first in cocktail shaking. Nothing to do but eat and lounge lizard, a mothbally tennis court and a saucer of a natural rock pool to play in, and a general feeling that you've stepped back in time and the art deco clocks are actually ticking a more civilized tock.

The sign on the island reads 'England 362 metres' and once the tide has closed in on two sides of the strip of sand between you and Bigbury-on-Sea, there is no escape save via the only working sea tractor in the world or a long and obligation filled relationship with Jacques Cousteau.

Jack and I took the train from Paddington with Adam and his best friend Will, who have worked out a double act called 'synchronized stupidity' which passed the time, initially hilariously and finally infuriatingly till Exeter gave way to lovely rolling scenery.

On the journey I read, as I ritualistically do on train journeys, *Private Eye*. In 'Pseuds Corner' was a contribution from, I believe, *Tatler*, that well-known periodical for the proletariat, featuring Derek Nimmo on the only way to eat oysters. This involved strapping a bottle of Moët to your leg, then swimming out from Cap Ferrat to a tiny rock where you presumably let the little blighter slide down one side of your throat, the champers down the other and taste both afterwards. This is wildly inaccurate quoting, but you get the picture. Knowing and revering Lord Nimmeau of Mersey as I do, and being convinced that his adorable octogenarian chauffeur, John, was probably swimming behind him with a cold chicken and some asparagus in aspic balanced on a linen napkin on his peaked bathing hat, I read out this article with some relish. Knowing also that we would be working together later in the year, I tore out the cutting and secreted it gleefully about my person for regurgitation at the perfect moment. Like a quiet teabreak after a double speed dash through Acts I and II. I glanced at the list of contributors to see if I recognized who'd sent in the snippet, but no showbiz bell rang.

The arrangement was that we'd be picked up by a man in a maroon jacket. This somewhat George Smiley arrangement was just us being absurdly spoilt, since you can easily change to Totnes and take a short taxi ride, or fly from Heathrow to Plymouth or, if the mood takes you and you've recently won a lottery, fly 'Castle Air' *direct* to the island – by helicopter.

The maroon jacket (which turned out to be white with a red tie) drove us fifteen miles to Bigbury Bay, one of the most unsightly spots in Europe, and that's *not* in *Esquire*, with one stop at the Pickwick Pub to forewarn the sea tractor to stand by for four weary travellers, two synchronizing stupidly and two wondering why the hell they'd brought two suitcases for three days. Well the brochure said to dress for dinner and you never know! Cocktail gówns and beaded evening bags require space! And then there were *my* clothes.

The sea tractor has five foot high wheels, a staircase, a large orange-box to sit on top in, and fills one with the urge to sing 'Didn't we have a luverly time the day we went to Bangor'.

The hotel gleaming white with a fretwork of eau de nil window sills, was built in the Twenties by a music-hall star called George Chirgwin, known as 'the white-eyed Kaffir'. I'd encountered the name five years ago, in a programme of monologues. The late, and rather underrated actor Ronald Lacey, clad in pierrot costume, had appeared as Chirgwin in black face with a diamond of white over one eye and had broken my heart with a rendering of 'My Fiddle is My Sweetheart' sung to a six inch violin. So when I read a blurb in a glossy about the restoration and ropening by Tony and Bea Porter of the formerly famous society retreat, where the Prince took his illicit liaisons and Coward took the waters, I knew I was fated to be fêted there.

At close sight the hotel is cosier and slightly more rundown than I'd expected but only in a way which I personally find enchanting. It looks as if people live in it. A magnificent peacock-domed sun lounge on two levels joined by a double staircase yielded up the tea and scones whilst Thirties music by the 'Pennies from Devon' serenaded us at a discreet pitch.

Lloyd Loom chairs loomed and Clarice Cliff pottery pottered about in walnut burr sideboards. Every stick of furniture from the peach framed mirrors to the sugar tongs is authentic, lovingly and painstakingly collected by Tony and Bea on their one day off a week. Creating the essence of the period is the essence of their creation.

Our suite, the specially requested Chirgwin Suite,

was filled with enough uncut moquette, marquetry table nests and fan shaped wall-lights, to fill me with flapper-like glee and – wonder of wonders – a hotel with double beds! And a bolster! I was going to have to watch it or I'd become a statistic in a back number of *Esquire*!

We agreed that the boys would wander round the hotel whilst we wandered round the island, then we'd reverse it and meet up back in the morning room. This a large checker-floored terraced room, with dramatic views of the sea and coast, which gives way to a wood-pannelled ship's prow of a room with windows all aslant in which the boys fell into a Monopoly rally which lasted for the duration. But only when the sun shone outside. Jack and I climbed up to the Ruer's ruin, a stone-walled hut on the crest of the hill in which in olden times lurked the Ruer himself. His job – and I guess it was a good job in its day – was to watch the waters for signs of frothing. The frothing indicated that the pilchards had arrived and the Ruer would then run down the hill shouting stuff like 'Pilchards Ahoy! Pilchards Ahoy! Get your butts off the scrumpy vats and see if you can get the little buggers to swim into the tins!'

Nowadays, the pilchards, like the rest of us, have chosen to follow the Gulf Stream to warmer climes, but the pub defiantly remains 'The Pilchard's Arms' as opposed to the 'Monkfish Kebaberie'. Looking down, the hotel really looked like a Thirties cruise ship about to be launched by darling Boo with a bottle of Bollinger wrapped in an organza necktie.

We strolled back for a little hectic tennis – damp balls and intrusive foliage – and a short walk on the beach to the mossy rocks to savour the dusk falling all around each round ended, square paned window of the hotel. There's a shop in the basement selling Art Deco artefacts and I promised myself as we travelled suite-wards in the tiny chrome and glass elevator, that tomorrow was treats day.

We dressed carefully for dinner in the 'Ballroom', the boys grumblingly donning suits and slaughtering each other with their ties and assembled in the cocktail bar for something lethal. There was one other couple in there, young, fair-haired and friendly and we fell into conversation with them. We discussed, as one does, the routes which had brought us to the same cocktail shaker and the various vagaries on board. It will come as no surprise to the readers of Arthur Koestler's works that Hannah, the bubbly female half of the pair, was the person who had sent in to the *Eye* the afore-mentioned piece of Pseud. Small island, isn't it?

Finally, pausing only to check oneself in the multi-mirror tiled pillars into the dining room, again built on the lines of a liner and decorated in the saxe-blue and cream of that most social and sociable of eras, we hit the dining room. Dinner was excellent, carrot and basil soup labelled delicious by man, boy and Mother alike and fish in Pernod and butter sauce which actually had me watery eyed with pleasure. All around on four sides, the water twinkled, the stars twinkled, the lights of Salcombe twinkled – and

I have to tell you my husband began to show distinct signs of twinkling too.

Pause for imaginations to work undertime. Discreet cough . . .

Breakfast was the real thing. On hols we are serious breakfasters. Porridge, poached eggs, kippers and masses of hot buttered toast. Famous Five stuff. We learned that Agatha Christie came here to write *Ten Little In* . . . er, ten little ethnic minorities, and I'm sure if I'd stayed there a few more days I'd have been inspired to write ten more.

Day two was misty and cool and we strolled across the beach to the mouth of the river and back to Bigbury to take a drive with Ann from the Devon tourist board into Salcombe's meandering and crowded lanes. Amidst an alarming number of Cap'n Birdseye clones we saw off fresh plaice and chips in the Spinnaker restaurant and watched terracotta sailed yachts glide over marine blue water. A fair amount of 'Is it *her* or isn't it?' filtered in my direction and I began to have withdrawal cravings for the Chirgwin suite.

'Wouldn't you like to change your face?' asked Ann.

'Totally,' I replied. 'But I'd still need people to see it and say is it *her* or isn't it?'

We actually visited a shire horse and falconry centre – oh yes, *right* up my street! Actually it was fun and I shall treasure for ever the moment when, during a demonstration, a kestrel flew into the crowd and the trainer said 'Don't be afraid. He likes little girls.' (Pause) 'Between two slices of bread.'

Dinner that night was accompanied by an accompanist who gave us Gershwin and Porter with our chicken terrine in three fruit coulis and baked salmon in delicious peppery juices. I longed to dance, but, as usual in my family, I was the only one who did. Snooker and table tennis were more what the boys had in mind so we wrinklies joined other wrinklies in the Palm Court Bar and felt no pain at all.

We left by sea tractor the next day at 11.00 after relieving ourselves of a decent supply of dosh in the downstairs shop and saying goodbye to Tony and Bea, desperately trying to drag themselves off the island for their day off. I can understand why. I don't think I've described the essence of Burgh Island well enough. It's difficult to sum up a feeling. I've visited several hotels in Cannes, Antibes and Juan les Pins – but it's Burgh Island I keep bragging about. Go. Travel the 362 metres. Then just lie back and *don't* think of England.

Altered States

'You wanna cab ma'am?' snapped the porter at Kennedy Airport as Julia McKenzie and I tried to force our trolley wheels in a direction they clearly didn't want to go.'

'Er ... yes – thank you, but don't we have to wait?'

'No way.' He took charge of my luggage and forged relentlessly past the queue, leaving me lurching along behind. 'Jules,' I stage-whispered. 'I've only got ten dollars – have you got anything smaller?' She didn't have, so as he reached the front of the cab rank, I leaned over and slipped the note into his hand. At which point all hell broke out. The automatic doors flew open and out barged two plain-clothed, walkie-talkie clutching security robo-cops yelling 'Hold it right there!' Instantly, our nice friendly 'porter' vanished into polluted air and the two guys turned on *me* yelling 'THIS IS EXACTLY WHAT WE'RE TRYING TO AVOID! JESUS! DID YOU COME THROUGH VIP? I MEAN *THIS* IS EXACTLY WHAT ... DID YOU? HUH?' I opened my mouth and nothing came out. Jeremy Beadle wasn't even about.

Julia spoke for me 'Yes, we came with the VIP office. She left us at the doorway and ...' 'JESUS! did you hear that?' then, into his handset, 'GET ME SECURITY – NOW – JESUS, THESE GUYS – OK. OK. YOU'RE IN NEW YORK, OK? These guys hang around airports to steal your baggage OK? Whadya give him?'

I opened my mouth again and Julia's voice said 'Ten dollars.'

'JESUS,' he barked and disappeared through the automatic doors with a mechanical hiss and a cushioned thud. We looked at each other. I'd been on American soil for twelve minutes, in which time I'd almost lost all my luggage and tipped the thief ten dollars for trying to take it. Sitting in the cab, driven by a taciturn White Russian, we started to giggle.

What were we doing there? I was seeing a play, Neil Simon's *Lost in Yonkers*, which I was set to do in the West End and researching a travel article on the Catskills Mountains and Julia was checking out a theatre where she hoped to direct a musical. On paper that is. In fact, what we were doing was 'skyving off'. Leaving it all behind – husbands, dogs, dependants, swotting kids, All Quiet On The West

End Front Agents. Going off tatts, up west, girls together – one bite of the Big Apple so far and, already, we'd found the worm.

Our friends, the Taffners had, with wild generosity, lent us an apartment on West 57th Street. It was warm and snug with real tea-bags and we unpacked and watched TV sinfully from our beds. The Sunday Godslot slots were playing and the Reverend Tilson was expanding his message of redemption: 'Send me your money and your success in life is guaranteed. I will then send you a piece of this cloth (close-up cloth) which ah have personally blessed.' Cut to film of Sandra and Don with their handicapped child, Chad. Apparently, since sending their last few dollars to the Reverend Tilson, at a time when they were homeless, jobless, penniless and unable to cope with Chad, they have miraculously found a nice, large family house, a job for Don and an incredible improvement in Chad's disability. All this from 112 inches of Crimplene!

Later we picked up food and Campari and sodas from the neighbourhood deli. 'Winter is unwilling to release us from its grip, ma'am,' said the doorman, who was Irish and had a propensity for saying such things. Indeed, the following day was St Patrick's Day and there was to be a seven hour parade.

'You girls already made two big mistakes,' said producer Manny Azenberg down the phone. 'New York on St Patrick's and the Catskills out of season. Don't go,' he continued. 'We'll take you to see the *Catskills on Broadway* revue and that will tell you everything you need to know about the area. With laughs. And stay away from the parade – there's vomit everywhere – everyone hates it, even the Irish.'

It also seemed the parade was under threat from The Irish Gay and Lesbian Society who had been prevented from marching. I *think* their organization was called DILGO. Concerned but undaunted, we headed for the Plaza Hotel to watch the parade over brunch and from a distance. I interrupted the first managerish person I saw to learn they didn't serve brunch. It was only as I thanked him Englishly that I realized the person he'd been talking to was his boss, one Donald Trump. Taller and pinker, since you ask.

Outside, the eighteenth group of bagpipes was just marching past and we nervously joined the crowds at the barricades in time to see the 'Irish Argentinian Association' walk past. All *six* of them, including a large, middle-aged woman wearing an ill-fitting ballgown in eggshell blue and long black braids. All six looked a bit sheepish.

Julia wanted earplugs against the traffic, earrings for the First Night party and tights for propriety, so we braved both the upcoming blizzard and Bloomingdales. Then we scuttled back through the barricades towards 57th Street to dress for our first 'First Night'. Foyers in New York are small and cramped, unlike most of our yawning lobbies, so the likes of Harrison Ford, Lauren Bacall, Jule Styne, Stephen Sondheim and, wraith-like in black on black, Darryl Hannah, were outside jamming the sidewalk. Afterwards we attended one of the legendary first night parties where Frank Rich's *New York Times* notice comes out at 11.30 and the party empties at 11.35. Very sobering, I can tell you. Who'd want to be in a theatre play? The following night we saw *Lost in Yonkers* and I remembered who'd want to be. Me. I laughed till I cried, cried till I laughed and had nothing to mop up the tears save Julia's cashmere wrap.

The following day I went to the Russian Tea Room where I had blintzes with sour cream and caviar. I'm mortified to tell you I ate *six*. My best white wool dress began to shrink on me as I sat there. Opposite, against the dazzling ruby red and gold decor, sat Carol Channing. Nobody looks intentionally like Carol Channing. I'd love her to see herself. In the next booth, no, straight up, scout's honour, sat Woody Allen. Mr Apple himself. I'd read somewhere that he doesn't like to be looked at – in fact an actor friend once told me he'd had an audition for one of his films and had been specifically instructed not, under any circumstances, to address Mr Allen, although Mr Allen would be in the room. He did the audition then, on his way out, unable to resist it, made so bold as to congratulate Mr Allen on his last movie – at which point Mr Allen made a small sound, jumped up and fled the room. My friend, oddly enough, didn't get the role. Consequently, I spent the whole lunch *not* looking at Woody Allen. I'm sure it was my imagination but I *felt* he was a bit peeved.

Afterwards I went to the Lincoln Center where, in a small room, I put on earphones and was plugged into the video of *Lost in Yonkers* recorded live on stage with the original cast. I had meant to make comparisons. Instead I got sucked inside the play in a way which only the use of 'close-ups' can do for you and sat weeping long after the other TV-monitor watching people had left for home and the staff were dying to do the same. With this marvellous, sub-scription-based scheme, you can see all the Broadway shows you thought you'd missed for ever – and no one laughs or shifts around or gets bleeped by their office. It's what I call a real night in. Bleary-eyed I collapsed at the apartment of actor friend Simon Jones, whose three year old son, Timothy, is, seriously now, the most wonderful child ever born. The TV was playing Neil Simon's *Broadway Bound*. I'd had it – I spent the evening with Timmy, who is very well-cast and almost as funny.

That night we saw the hit revue *The Catskills on Broadway* in the company of Manny and Neil Simon (by now Ms McKenzie and I in dire danger of having our heads turned at least 90 degrees). One of the comics, Mal Z Lawrence, was so funny, so surreally, dangerously funny, that I feared for my life. 'If he doesn't stop, I'm going to lose both bladder control and my next job,' I whispered to Jules. Afterwards, we were winded and Neil Simon had to go to the restroom to wash his eyes. Can you define what makes someone so funny? The man looked like a roadie for Tom Jones, bald head, pigtail, sharp suit, strange balletic movements and a control of his audience which verges on the hypnotic. Afterwards the cast members collected at the back of the audience for Aids charities and one of them told me they are heading for London. Prepare to die!

Did I tell you we lunched with Dolores Gray? Julia had worked with the legendary Hollywood actress in Sondheim's *Follies*. I went along 'cos, as you'll have noticed from the relentless namedropping that's been going on for some paragraphs, I'm star struck. Her apartment is a small but perfect replica of Fontainebleau. All in dusty pink. It's her pride and her passion and everything has to be hand finished. The previous evening and most of the night had been spent in a wild and wonderful way – and not the way you're thinking of. No, she'd spent it making a tray. A solid wood galleried tray on which to serve us drinks. It seemed that her favourite English butler's tray had been damaged so, rather than serve us champagne on, say, just a tray, she went out and bought wood, varnish, a small saw and a mitre-box and stayed up all night dove-tailing until she'd made a replica. It took a while to find it since she'd left it to dry in the piano stool, but that only heightened the drama of its appearance. What a lady – and what a story she had to tell if someone could just pin her to a chair and make her spill it.

We lunched at the Blue Train in Bloomingdales, a reproduction of the famous French train with brass luggage racks and, strangely, plush dark green decor and I almost fell out of my Bergère when she told us

Bob Hope's one-liner in the men's room to the, apparently, vastly endowed Forrest Tucker: 'Gee, aren't you afraid that thing's gonna turn on you one day?'

'Gee, it's a shame you're here right *now*,' said Hope, the Sullivan County PR lady on the line to our New York apartment. 'Y'see we're kinda in between seasons and ... uh, well, the Sullivan County *Museum* may be open and er ... there could be cross-country skiing – so long as it doesn't rain. The ski lifts have closed down right now, but the maple syrup farm should be open ... You see, I only just took over from Margot and ... I wonder, are you at all innerested in fly fishing?'

I must confess that all I was innerested in right then was staying on 57th Street, turning up the heat, and steadily demolishing the seven different kinds of bagels we'd just bought in the deli.

Let me retrace my steps. 'How would you like to do the Jewish Alps?' said the travel editor of the *Daily Telegraph* a few weeks earlier.

'Only if I can take a token Gentile,' replied I, sharp as a tack. The thought of staying at a Catskills resort hotel just an hour and a half from New York, overdosing on the food my mother told me *her* mother used to make, was an offer I could only accept. My husband donned his 'but I've already had a week's holiday this year' look, so I offered the package to my little chum Jules.

'It was a fact handed down from his ancestor the

historian that the Catskill Mountains had always
been haunted by strange beings.' So wrote Washington Irving in his timeless tale of time-warp *Rip
Van Winkle*, the story of a simple man who slept
whilst history changed around him. A prophetic
metaphor for the area, as it happens. I doubt though
whether the beings Mr Irving had in mind were any
stranger than myself and Julia checking ourselves
into Kutshers Country Club, in the very heart of the
Catskills 'always in season' Mountains, in the guise
of two serious investigative journalists.

Aside from 'Rip', my knowledge of the Catskills
leaned heavily on a misspent youth collecting
Motion Picture mags: 'Eddie 'n' Liz in Grossingers
Love Nest – Jenny Grossinger defends decision to
shelter Liz 'n' Debbie's ex in Catskills Honeymoon
Suite'. Several husbands later (Liz's, not mine), I
was intrigued to read that this beautiful, mountain-
ous, lake-peppered area of New York State had
become popular in the Twenties and Thirties as a
bolt hole for underprivileged and ethnically
restricted New York families who would never
otherwise have smelled any grass but butcher's or
swum in anything other than a hydrant under a fire
escape. The hotels and boarding houses became a
sort of Kosher Butlins. Not exclusively Jewish; some
hotels were all Italian, some Irish, some German but
on the whole the skill of these cats was to provide a
lot of what had been left behind. With fresh air and
fun. One of its most famous residents, alas no longer
performing, was Peg Leg Bates, the one-legged tap

dancer. I'd have killed to see him.

Comedians like Danny Kaye, Jack Benny and Jackie Mason began as 'tumelers' in the resort hotels. The equivalent of redcoats, they would entertain by the pool by day, tell jokes on stage by night and dance with the wallflowers by order of the management.

Nowadays, the Catskills, like the rest of us, is in a recessive period, trying to decide what to *be*. In high season, the lakes, excellent golf courses, ice rinks, tennis schools and kids' camps are chock-a-block, but the atmosphere has changed, along with the old clientele who now perhaps ski in Aspen or, if the dollar and the snow holds, in Gstaad. Still, the hotels are glorious, in a slightly faded, overblown Fifties way, which makes them irresistible to me. I like to feel ghosts.

The dining rooms are a movable feast, in several senses of both words. The Concorde, which is too large and impersonal for my taste, at most can take 3,000. Walls come and go to make seating for thousands or handfuls of diners. At Kutshers, a wedding party and a barmitzvah were scarcely noticeable as Julia and I chomped our way through a starter of chopped liver, herring, egg and onion, coleslaw, and cream cheese and smoked salmon which could have fed Russia. Sylvia, our larger than loaf and twice as wry *maître d'* who hailed, twenty years ago, from Enfield, took us over, mothered and force fed us. 'You don't know whether to have the oriental beef or the coq au vin – watsamadderwityou? Have both. Louis!' Twenty seconds later the dangerously hot dishes hit the deck, and, yes, I obediently ate both. Followed by Clover Honey Cake. Would I lie to you?'

Helen and Milton Kutsher, eating customarily at their family table, are dear, kind people and their memories are precise and fascinating. I'm still savouring the moment when Louis, a waiter of twenty years' standing, slipped Milton a forbidden biscuit and accompanied it, quite unconsciously, with a kiss on the boss's head. I mean we are talking *family* hotel here. Julia and I were instantly at home and didn't relish leaving without a return booking. If you want your privacy I'm sure you can get it – there are eighteen hole golf courses outside the windows, more lakes than you can fly fish through, every kind of court from volleyball through, probably, to King Arthur's, bridge, pools, saunas and a programme for kids which keeps them organized from dawn to dusk, when you get them back just as you like 'em - pink and exhausted. All this plus three groaning meals a day and two shows a night thrown in. For 73 dollars a day, off season. Can you afford to miss it?

Now, Chic it ain't. People do dress up but mostly into scenes from *La Dolce Vita.* There is nothing in the downstairs shop, and I mean *nothing* that ain't appliquéd . . . and then some. Here a bead, there a sequin, everywhere a rhinestone, it was like being inside Bet Lynch's brain. However, you will never feel slimmer than you do in the Catskills. Compared to some of the *tochases* we saw encased in leggings, McKenzie and I are bulimics. And the company varies, we met some charming New Yorkers, real high flyers who came because they loved the beautiful countryside, appreciated the value and felt comfortable with the ambience.

The legendary nightclub entertainment was a bit skimpy due more to our bad timing than the comics, but Kutshers' Joanne Engel provided an hour's cabaret of polished good nature to an audience largely consisting of leftover wedding guests waving luminous neck-rings and whining along to the best tunes. Coming shortly we are told are Steve 'n' Eydie, The Everlys and Catskills' kitten, Joan Rivers. I wish *we* were.

Most of the local attractions, like the Monticello racetrack and the Fly Fishing Centre, were closed but we saw, and wished we hadn't, the Apollo Shopping Centre and some mouth-watering antique shops. I was levered protesting out of 'Memories' in Parkville, clutching an American quilt, china, an old camera and more. All I needed now was another suitcase. That evening we dined royally at 'The Old Homestead' where they serve twenty-three ounce steaks. 'But that's a cow,' said Julia and settled instead for succulent lobster claws, baked potatoes and a pecan pie to commit a federal offence for. The friendliness, the genuine pleasure in serving you 'somp'n good' in this neck of the woods is a mark of a classless society which we can only make speeches about. Likewise, when 'Marge' showed us around her beloved Sullivan County Museum and told us she'd scrubbed the boards of the old schoolroom herself to turn it into a charming, unpretentious record of the County's history, she did it with a pride which made my eyes prickle. 'Now here's the canal bridge where the barges filled with coal used to sail through . . . and see, here's where the poor kids used to shout abuse at the bargeman so's he'd throw coal at them, and that way' – pause for dramatic effect – 'they could take it home for kindling!'

Finally, in temperatures of sub-zero, we stood by the Maple Syrup Farm commiserating with the farmer. 'Sorry, nope, the sap's not rising today.'

'God, I know that feeling,' I told him through defrosting teeth. Apparently, in twenty years there'll be no maple syrup to sap because of pollution killing off trees. World maple syrup extinction. Accordingly, we bought between us six large and still warm flagons and some Maple Mousse for Sylvie. Memo: must get that suitcase.

On our final day, we visited 'The Guest House'. I'd asked Hope, the PR lady, to take me to a small inn, as a contrast to the multi-lobbied opulence and sprawling grounds of Kutshers but even she wasn't prepared for the adventure this became. We drove to Liberty County with the sun breaking across the vast thawing landscape. Most of my knowledge of upstate America is based on movies set in small towns where the gaps between the houses are as high as an elephant's thigh – the impression is even more so when you visit. Houses are scattered about, like chalets on a Swiss mountain, each one individual and original. The small towns are one street small

towns, not all that far removed from *Little Women*.
One post office, one drug store, one tiny clapboard
church ... and no suitcase store. Rip Van Winkle
could wake up now and not think he'd taken
L-Dopa. The 'Guest House' was marked by no
garish sign. Just a long discreet driveway to an
L-shaped, wooden house with a deep chalet roof at
the door of which stood an even more L-egant figure
in Missoni and mink, emeralds sparkling in the mid-
day sun.

'Hello and velcome to "The Guest House",'
purred the proprietress as Julia and I pulled our
track suits over our hips and flailed at our wind-
scrunched hair. 'My name is Andrea, let me show
you around "The Guest House" and then ve shall
have lunch over at *my* house, yes?' Well. Yes. The
four bedrooms and beamed living room were furn-
ished exquisitely in the manner of the second home
of an exiled European monarch. The decor was
casually elegant, the log fired grate just waiting for
its cue to crackle, low coffee tables sated with *Horse
and Hound* and *Field* mags, rugs, drapes, antiques,
everything coordinated – the best of American and
European Country House chic, with the odd salute
to chinoiserie thrown in. The Honeymoon Suite
made you hanker after remarriage, something our
hostess informed us she'd done several times before
finding her present spouse, whose Godparents,
silver-framed on the piano, appeared to be our very
own Queen Mother and her late husband. This was
no ordinary inn and Andrea – 'I advise my guests

where to eat dinner. You have to *earn* your place at my table.' – was no ordinary landlady. Over lunch in her own country house, five minutes away by bridge over the Willowemoc river, she revealed that she had in her time produced movies, interviewed Saddam Hussein ('Charming. A pig, but charming.') and best of all was 'a doctor *manqué*, which is how I discovered the crucial evidence for Klaus's Appeal,' at which point the cent dropped and I realized that this landlady was none other than Andrea Reynolds, former girlfriend of Klaus von Bülow. I could hardly wait to get to the video shop.

So if you fancy earning your place at a really classy joint where fly fishing, hunting, swimming and complimentary English tea abound and you get to rub shoulders with the great and the near great by proxy – you know vere to go,

Thus it was a very shiny-eyed pair of thespians posing as investigative journalists who sped back to their large, airy rooms at Kutshers to swim, shower and change and bid not goodbye but *au revoir*. Oh yes. I shall return. Perhaps with my mother and perhaps not in the high season – just for the beauty of the landscape, the walks, the outdoor life and, above all, the folks. To say hello again to Helen and Milton, Warren the porter, Louis and Sylvia, who ran after our departing forms waving two boxes of Danish 'for the joiney – it couldn't hoit'.

Someday soon, someone with wads of greenbacks will legalize gambling and thus transform the 'blue and purple crown of glory' that is the Catskills.

They'll put a CentreParc on the old Grossingers site and install 'Disney Vallee'. Do yourselves a favour, see it whilst it's as it is – 'It can't hoit'.

New York is built on granite and they say this gives you energy. Let me describe our last day. Packing from seven till eight, phone calls till *I Love Lucy* which simply improves with my age, then out for corn beef hash and coffee in the nearest deli. Over to the Manhattan Theater Club for Julia to see the space for her revue, cab to the *shmatta* (garment) area where we overdose on the knits, back to Bloomingdales to buy a suitcase to transport it all home, then over to the Shubert Theater for a matinée of the new old Gershwin Musical *Crazy For You*, cab to Jim Dale's Park Avenue apartment – all Art Nouveau and 'Art to Wear' on the walls – for a 'scream tea' about the old days, and a quick wave off as Dan Taffner's black-windowed double limo swept us silently to Kennedy for the seven o'clock flight home. Energy? Were we tired? I haven't been so tired since the delivery room. Or so happy. The ten days that shook the girls. U.S.

6

Filing Cabinet

Toujours Provinces

In 1990 I played The Royal Exchange Theatre in Manchester. It wasn't a long run. In fact it started at 11.30 am and it finished an hour later. However, it was very well received by the 750 ladies who made up the audience. They were not a tough house. I think if I'd read my way through the Florence Greenberg cookbook they'd have given me as good a reception, but I didn't. Only slightly daunted by the first totally in-the-round theatre I've played, with people sitting all round me at stage level and similarly two levels up, I soon realized that the best way to make a relationship with them was to walk around with my mobile mike, ringmaster style, until I tied myself up in knots. It was all good stuff, and sold a few copies of *Thank You for Having Me*.

The theatre's director, Braham Murray, was away on the day of my talk, so we didn't get the chance to renew an acquaintance which began in the mid-Sixties when he was a hungry young director and I was a drama student and not a bit hungry, thanks to the weekly food parcels from Hull. Braham's rather exotic girlfriend, Jasmina, was in my class at LAMDA, and he took some workshop classes with the students with a view of creating a show. In fact we spent a couple of merry but puzzling weeks putting together a revue about prunes. I'm quite serious. Prunes. The fruit world's visual answer to an excess of eggs.

Anyway, the idea was to re-evaluate the humble prune for an advertising agency. It didn't, on reflection, look like a great idea for a musical, although *See How They Run* might have been a nice alternative title. Then who's to say what a good subject for a musical is? 'Erm, hello Mr Macintosh, I wonder if you'd be at all interested in putting the feline poems of TS Eliot on stage, with all the cats played by ballet dancers and a pile of rubbish centre stage?'

'No I wouldn't. Sod off and don't waste my time again.' Who's to say?

Actually, years later, driving through France with Jack, we happened upon the 'prunier' region of the Dordogne and were startled by the attention the wrinkled fruit was getting. Whole shops were devoted to their versatility. Elegantly wrapped, beribboned boxes, some heartshaped, some velvet, some multi-layered – 'Ooh la la, Simone, regard lui – un autre pruneau'. Sweet prunes, savoury prunes, prunes in brandy, prunes in liqueur, prunes nestling in straw beds, prunes wrapped in candied shells, in coconut caramel ... your humble Bridlington breakfast prune in every conceivable situ; except sitting, scatalogically, in a bowl with juice round them. Revelation. Only then did I bemoan the loss of that potential megabuck West End hit, *Prunes*, starring Dame Kiwi te Kanawa and Placido Domango and Lycheeano Pavarotti, book by William Shakes-pear, lyrics by Banana Moscouri, music by John Lemon and directed, of course, by Hal Quince!

'In the month of June, I softly croon, our favourite tune, while we kiss and share a prune.' Sheer bloody magic! Is it too late for a revival, I wonder?

But I digress. Flashback twenty years to the production that never was. Braham went on his way to becoming a first rate director and we LAMDA students went on to finish our drama courses without recourse to any further pruning. Just before the final end of term shows, in which I was to play Lucrece in the famous play, *The Rape of Lucrece* (lorra words, norra lorra laffs), we were all frantically writing letters to agents and casting directors: 'Dear Adsa Vincent, I am a third year student at LAMDA and I was wondering whether you would like tickets for the LAMDA production of *The Rape of Lucrece* in which I have the good fortune to play the Rapée.'

It occurred to me that perhaps I should write to out erstwhile director and invite him along. I wrote the letter, but having never seen his somewhat unusual name actually written down, I wrote 'Dear

Bra . . .' and left the rest to be filled in after consultation with his girlfriend at college the next day. Needless to say, I forgot to ask her, forgot what I'd written and posted the letter and, needless to say, a polite refusal note came back, headed 'Dear Mau'.

Twenty-five years went by for both of us and there I was in Manchester, addressing his Ladies Who Lunch, and there he wasn't. He was in London lunching with impresario Duncan Weldon, discussing the possibilities of a new West End production, perhaps a Pinero play. However, letters were exchanged afterwards, with careful spelling of each other's names, and dinner at 'Odette's' in Primrose Hill (Pruniers being all booked-up) was arranged for the next time he was in town.

It was tricky renewing a relationship that had never really been. Almost harder than starting from scratch. We were both a little nervous through the hors-d'oeuvres. Fortunately we soon discovered a mutual love of food, football and family, and after that we cared not a fig. He asked me to consider the title role in Pinero's *The Schoolmistress*. I had a fancy for Pinero because the National Theatre's production of *Trelawney of the Wells* had stayed in my mind so vividly and the finest comic performance I've ever seen was also in a Pinero play. It was Alastair Sim in *The Magistrate*.

I liked *The Schoolmistress*. My agent and my husband didn't. The producer, Duncan Weldon, was much keener to do *Hobson's Choice*, but I carried such strong memories of Julia McKenzie in the role that I doubted my capabilities to measure up to her.

Almost my favourite theatrical anecdote is Julia's experience of playing Maggie Hobson to Ronald Pickup's Willy Mossop. One night, well into the run, she came to the moment in the show when Maggie summons Willy from the basement to inform him that he has great skills as a cobbler and she intends him to be her husband. 'Willy,' she tells him, 'show me your hands,' and goes on to tell him that he has the hands of a craftsman.

On this particular night, she summoned him as usual, he poked his head out of the trapdoor and, bright as a button and twice as shiny, she rapped out the command: 'Hans, show me your Willy'!

Suffice it to say that the Willy in question shot back down the trapdoor and Maggie Hobson got uncommonly interested in the dusting of every article on the upstage mantelpiece.

The compromise play which then raised its not unattractive head was Pinero's comedy farce *The Cabinet Minister*. Almost exactly 100 years ago it opened to mixed reviews and approving audiences, but had scarcely been performed since. Michael Denison had adapted it for a touring production with his wife, Dulcie Gray, for Duncan, and Braham Murray had directed a very successful revival at the Royal Exchange theatre four years previously. He was dying to do it again.

It read very well. *The Cabinet Minister* of the title is Sir Julian Twombley a doddery MP with a younger and somewhat frivolous, countryborn wife,

Kitty, who is, unbeknown to him, leading him into financial ruin. A mismatch between their beautiful daughter and a mother-fixated Scottish lord is arranged, and a money-lender and his scheming sister are introduced to lead Kitty further and further into debt and despair. The denouement comes about by means of a disgraceful piece of insider-trading, and the whole, awful, snobbish family fail to receive their comeuppance. It is a cleverly worked plot and, although some of the dialogue is rather too straight for a regular farce, it has moments of sublime humour and a large dramatis personae who all have lovely, well-defined characters.

The person of an ethnic minority in the woodpile, as far as I could see, was that the money-lender, Joseph Lebanon, is described on his first entrance as 'An unctuous person of a most pronounced Semitic type', and his character then evolves as a brash, larger than life, East End, eye for the main chance, essentially naïve, man on the make. A bourgeois version of every other social climber in the play in fact.

I expressed my worry to Braham that the character could be perceived as anti-Semitic. He replied that, aside from Pinero's stage direction, there was no other reference to the man's ethnicity and that Pinero was himself a Jew, writing from the point of view of an outsider. Since he, Braham, was Jewish and the producer likewise, it seemed unlikely that any of us would wish to do a play which contained even suggested prejudice. To allay any doubts I may have had, he forwarded the national reviews from the production he'd done four years previously with Susan Fleetwood and Frank Thornton. I scoured them for anti-Semitic references. But found none.

Furthermore, Braham then phoned to say Derek Griffiths was interested in the role of Lebanon. After a pause of several seconds, I realized this was probably inspired casting. Griffiths, a superb black actor and comic, would play Lebanon as a Semitic businessman, as described by Pinero, but not specifically a Jewish one.

The choice was made. Kitty Twombley would suit me. She was pretentious, vain, snobbish but also skittish, warm and very entertaining. Her origins were humble and her over-whelming love of her 'precious chicks' (her two children) was her redeeming feature. Her tenacity almost outweighed her mendacity. I could see how I could play her. Also, after three years solo in *Re:Joyce*, it would be a wonderful change to be surrounded by actors. There was a cast of fourteen, three sets, dazzling costumes and a short tour before London. Added to which, we knew that the majority of the critics felt the play and its production deserved a London revival, so all should be well. And if you believe that then you probably believe carrots make you see in the dark and Guinness is good for you.

Unfortunately, Derek Griffiths decided to do a pantomime instead that year, and it was only a few weeks before we started rehearsals that we finally had our Joseph Lebanon in Teddy Kempner. My old sparring partner, Derek Nimmo, was to play the title role, Gwen Watford was to play his sister, the Dowager Dora, and Sara Kestelman the scheming Mrs Gaylustre, part lady, part dressmaker. I'd never met Gwen before but I'd loved her television work over the years, especially in the Charles Wood series *Don't Forget to Write*, which allowed her to use her exquisitely pained face to great comic effect. I might have known she would be one of the great gigglers of our time, and a rock of sanity and good humour in the company through good times and bad. Sara, I had known socially for years but never worked with. She is a great story-teller. I mean great. With almost perfect recall, she can recount events which make you feel like a fly on the wall in a long-vanished drama. I would sit spellbound through car journeys (we turned out to be neighbours), while she Scheherazaded her way through Hornsey and Holborn, her deep, mellow voice weaving spells which held me all the way to Waterloo, with the epilogue in the Old Vic car park.

Julia McCarthy and Malcolm Rennie were to play the Scots mother and son, Lady McPhail and Sir Colin. They had played the same roles in the last production in Manchester and they were perfect from day one. Hilarious. She, tiny, birdlike and tough as haggis; he, gawky, ginormous and gormless. Wee and Large.

And so to the first day of rehearsals, beginning with

the customary read-through of the script. I don't suppose the words 'read-through' hold the same sense of real terror for you as they do for me. For me the words are more or less synonymous with smear-test, root canal work and 'the VAT man will be calling Thursday.'

Actually I haven't had one for ages. A read-through I mean. 1987 *Wonderful Town*, Watford. That's the last time I sat down whey faced and icky with twenty or thirty quivering thespians and heard the equally icky-faced director say, 'well, there's nothing for it but to . . . er, read through it, really – is there?'

And you're always unprepared. No matter how many hours you've spent trying out your most comprehensive range of lilts, limps and lisps, it never quite comes out the way you've heard it in the privacy of your bed, your bathroom, your car and your local 'Curry Paradise'. And if it does come out in the right nasal cockney whine in Act I, then you can rest assured that by Act III it'll come out in a Welsh baritone.

Of course before you begin to actually read, there is the ritual of the greeting of the actors you have known, wished you hadn't known, once met at an audition for the PG Tips chimps' voices or once slept with on an overnight couchette from Perth after a particularly gruelling recording of *Martin Chuzzlewit* for Radio 4.

'Hı, I'm Maureen,' (they *know*. They've seen the ads)

'Yes Hello! I'm *Chris* – Jerry and Julian send huge amounts of love – I was with them at Stratford East in . . .'

'Oh great! How *are* they?' (*Who* are they?)

'Fine! Jules is just about to do a thing at the Beeb with Dame Judi and . . .'

'Hi *Darling*!' (We all call each other darling *not* because we're pretentious prats, although often we are, but because we're so nervous of making the wrong impression that we can't remember our *own* names let alone anyone else's.)

'Where are you sitting? God isn't this hell? It doesn't get any easier does it?' By now, coffee in polystyrene cups has wobbled into sight and thespians are cooing 'oooh biscuits! Hob-nobs greattt!' as though they had their last square meal when Gandhi did, instead of twelve minutes ago in Joe Allen's.

'Practical' food we call it – meaning edible as opposed to prop food. There's an old joke about two down-at-heel actors who meet in the street and one says he's going to audition for the part of the squire's manservant in say *The Wood Pigeon* by Sebastian Slog:

'But my dear fellow,' says the other, 'that's a terrible part – why are you going up for that?'

'Got to, old chap,' says actor one, 'there's a practical cake in Act III.'

Actors can't resist real food. It's a throwback from the days of the starving strolling mummer. A sort of collective sense mummary. And I speak as one who has watched Miriam Margoyles eat location scrambled eggs from the palm of her hand. 'Actors,' says Zero Mostel in *The Producers*. 'Animals! Did ya ever eat with one?'

Actually, ten years ago during the filming of my husband's play *Barmitzvah Boy*, the extras, mostly Jewish extras, were seated for long periods of time in front of plates of chopped liver. Every time they rehearsed, the director said 'Don't eat the chopped liver – just pretend until the take.' Each time he called 'action' before a rehearsal, the extras *ate* the chopped liver.

'I shan't tell you again,' screamed the director, by now down to his last *vat* of liver. 'The next time we do it, if anybody eats the chopped liver they're fired.'

'Action!' he shouted, whereupon one extra ate the chopped liver and was fired. I often wondered what he told his wife and kids. 'I was fired for eating liver.' Personally, I would have taken my case to an industrial tribunal. Bearing in mind that the liver was on the plate in front of him, that he was Jewish *and* an actor – I reckon he'd have been reinstated by any thinking court in the land.

So, back to the read-through. Names have been announced and forgotten. Greetings have been exchanged, Digestives dunked, and now the designer reveals the perfectly cute little doll's house model of a set to a largely myopic cast. Keenly we all crane forward. Some crouch around the very edges of the cardboard proscenium arch. Some young blade will ask a pointedly obvious question like 'er – and this would be a chair here, would it?' and 'is this floor functional?' and at the end of the demonstration of how the back flats lift to reveal a painted conservatory there will be a universal 'aaaah' of discovery, as in 'oh *that's* how they've solved the transition scene. Brilliant.'

Afterwards there will be a respectful pause, broken by a senior member of the company who will sum up the overwhelmed feelings of the cast in one carefully chosen phrase such as 'stunning, Brian', followed by a low respectful rhubarb of approval from the rest of us.

The same performance then takes place over costumes. Only here everyone cranes to look at everyone else's costumes to show they are interested in the design as a whole not just their own part of it. Invariably, by some sort of theatrical ESP, most of the ladies will be wearing more or less the same colours to the first rehearsal as the fragments of material in their designs. This will be remarked on and taken as a good omen for the production.

The director will then talk a little about the play and the social period in which it is set, and pass around a few books and pictures which each actor will be almost frothing with desire to see, will stare at for twenty seconds, pass on speedily, and never look at again. At this point routes taken from Ealing and Clapham to the rehearsal rooms and car parking facilities will be discussed as a last minute diversionary tactic. Finally the assembled cast open their scripts. The actors who only say 'Sir Paul and Lady Marjorie are in the conservatory, my Lord?' have marked their parts in translucent orange pen, and the ones who've not long been out of RADA have divided their scripts up into Battenberg sections of rulered lines to indicate beats, units, intentions, actions, motivations and fag breaks.

The ones who've been at it for rather longer are, coincidentally, all seated together, slightly apart from the younger ones – not for reasons of superiority, quite the reverse. They're scared that this time they'll be tumbled. This time all will be revealed. They can't act. They never could. The awards on the mantelpiece were a case of mistaken identity. The air is heavy with casual terror. There is a silence you could bite. To flee or not to flee? 'Sir Paul and Lady Marjorie are in the conservatory, my Lord?'

Quietly, almost self-effacingly, another two hairs on your head turn grey.

Rehearsals were the usual mixture of highs and highers with the odd trough thrown in for ballast. Derek Nimmo, as always, was the people-watchers' favourite viewing. Arriving in his chauffeur-driven Rolls, impeccably garbed in three piece Savile Row, Alpaca coat and, on one glorious occasion, bowler hat, he fitted us in between breakfast meetings with the Jakartan Ambassador, lunch with a couple of Sirs and a Viscount at the Garrick and cocktails at the first, invitation only, gallery opening of the evening. The corner of the definitely community-centred rehearsal room was turned into his mini-office and his mobile phone was strategically placed so as not to interfere too much with the denouement scene in Act III. His energy is probably enough to fuel Sellafield and there'd be a lot less falling-out.

Derek's chauffeur, John, is eighty-two and a good deal more titled than many of Derek's lunch dates. He drives the Roller and butles for Derek and Pat, often it must be said at virtually the same time, because he has a relish for good old-fashioned service and he likes the outfits. He has been known to drive guests to Château Nimmeau in his chauffeuring gear, then nip through the garage, change into butler's gear and welcome the guests into the withdrawing room. He has a papery, wafer-thin elegance and I never see him without sinking into a deep and respectful curtsy. Since I only ever see him drawing up in the Roller or leaving in the Roller, I invariably end up curtsying in the street, giving the impression of someone with a deep respect for parking meters. Ideally, John should have been played by the late, great Alastair Sim and I'm not sure that even he, genius though he was, could have fully conveyed the glorious moment when, en route to our first touring date in Bath, John took the turning to Bristol instead and, when Derek called out to tell him he'd done so, hollered back 'Don't *shout* at me, sir. It makes my deaf-aid vibrate!'

Back at rehearsals the blocking – deciding on the actual movement in each scene – took days as we all expressed our insecurities by flexing new muscles,

objecting to the directional suggestions and studying
the script intensely with over-furrowed brows. This
goes on for a week and the furrowed brows go home
with you each evening. Notes like 'No room yet for
me to invent' and 'More blocking. I'm unsure. And
blocked.' 'I put on a long skirt and prayed for
inspiration', 'Gwen and Sara are so good – help!'.
Then, on Friday, the 13th, 'At last, a decent lunch
in the Young Vic. We all had a hoot over Malcolm
Rennie's working with Hylda Baker stories. She
once told him to buy a bottle of wine for the
company (fifteen people) and gave him a pound
from her stocking-top to pay for it! Derek very
excited with a find, in the Garrick Club, of the
original Pinero prompt copy of the play. It's full of
bits of business and D is determined to get them all
in. Braham just as determined to leave 'em out.

'This afternoon I paced like a panther, dropped
my inhibitions and let rip. Lots of laughs all round.
Relaxed company suddenly as Tim Wallers, lovely
funny actor attempts to say the word "Strathspey" at
least eight times and Melanie Thaw and I become
incapacitated. The spade work is done. Braham's in
control. We can afford to laugh. Good.'

One fear hung in the air, Julia McCarthy –
normally as strong as a very small ox, unsinkable and
unflappable – was not well. The chest infection for
which she was receiving antibiotics, wouldn't shift.
Everyone suggested everything (actors being what
they are, we all had at least six alternative practitioners apiece) but she continued to bark and

wheeze and the effort of keeping up a strong front was knocking her back.

The Scottish dance had to be rehearsed as often as possible and, in spite of the added stimulus of Mr Nimmo wearing his own tartan trews for practice clothes, it was hard for Julia to keep up her spirits. Just a week before we were due to leave for Plymouth, she was sent for X-rays and blood tests and, horribly and inevitably, she arrived one day to tell us that she not only had cancer but it was a secondary cancer. They had no idea where the first one was.

Julia was made of strong Scottish stock and she was not going to be beaten at the first hurdle. We had all known her at varying times. I had first trodden the boards with her at the Old Vic in 1971 in *The Captain from Kopenik* with Paul Schofield. I took over the part of 'lady on a bench in park' from someone who'd moved on to bigger things. Julia was another old, black-clad lady. Our nightly contact was brief, but her sweetness, jollity and the formidable strength in her tiny frame made a lasting impression on me. The cast members who'd been in Braham's original Manchester production all adored her and those who had just begun to know her in these rehearsals already felt they'd known her for ever.

Her understudy was also my understudy *and*, would you believe, Gwen's understudy. The understudy rehearsals were absurd, with people dodging around the stage, talking to themselves like a Danny Kaye movie. Paula Topham was up to the task. A calm, steady, handsome and extremely talented actress in her own right, she prepared herself to rehearse and open the show in Plymouth until Julia felt strong enough to return after her biopsy. We all hugged and kissed Julia and sincerely meant our shouts of 'Now you better bloody well *be* there' when she left rehearsals, but inside we all were terribly aware of her increasing frailty.

Plymouth and the Grand Hotel were breezy and welcoming and there is always a 'ping' of excitement on entering a new theatre in a new town. The Theatre Royal were making our sets and costumes and fittings were required with designer Terry Emery and the Theatre's chief dressmaker, Alex. Gwen and I would breakfast each morning in the narrow veranda which overlooked the Solent, silent, she with the full English and the *Daily Mail*, me with yoghurt and the *Guardian*, perfect compatibility. At rehearsals, Paula was word perfect and, though twenty years too young, giving an excellent version of the Scottish matriarch. Julia was scheduled to arrive in time for the dress rehearsal and first preview. Any crises we had as a company paled into insignificance besides waiting for news on her condition. Nightly telephone calls relayed the news that she was feeling stronger like the true 'pro' she was, raring to go.

My wig arrived from London. My brown wig. The one that was supposed to be blonde. The tight, frizzy schoolmarm's wig that was supposed to be in soft sculptured Victorian loops. Keep calm,

Maureen. It really doesn't matter that you look like Miss Beale and the back-end of Miss Buss, so long as you remember your lines and don't fall over the footstool. Mercifully, Danutia, who works part-time in the wig room, was a trained wig maker and she and Kim, our hairdresser, gritted their tailcombs and washed, bleached and reset the offending and extremely expensive item, and it came out just perfect.

The stage was a wide thrust and the theatre quite modern, but the Act I set, a stunning white wrought-iron and glass conservatory looked well in the space. The costumes were a glorious froth of apricot and cream organza, lilac satin and pink and russet voile, beneath which the boned and laced corsets creaked and whined maliciously. There were bum rolls and a boned crinoline cage and french knickers and I found myself wondering how on earth the next generation was ever procreated.

The technical rehearsal was inevitably endless and, as usual, the play went out of the window whilst we struggled with doors which mysteriously have real knobs on them, open and close therefore much more slowly than the Marcel Marceau variety we've grown to know and depend upon.

It was hot. My corsets had to be peeled off my slippery skin at the end of the run. My dresser was an angel who anticipated my every need. She became my mother, without the familiar traits, and I'd forgotten that I'm one too, until the evidence arrived in the shape of two beautiful, clean, perfect children and their gloriously weathered father.

On our last free evening, we tried to get in to see the Royal Naval Barracks, *HMS Drake*, where Jack was stationed during his National Service, but in spite of a lot of eyelash fluttering and telephone gestures, they were having none of us, dangerous looking quartet that we were. After they'd gone, however, I was privileged to join Mr Nimmo at a dinner party on *HMS Drake*.

Nimmo was a guest, for the week, of the Captain, David Wixon, and his wife – Poppet. On arrival he was leaning down to bring out his baggage from his Roller when a lady Wren, rather over-enthusiastically, slammed down the boot on his head and he had to be led to a comfortable chair until the stars ceased to shine. I told him she was probably angling for promotion. The party was incredibly glamorous, with much withdrawing and circulating the kind of silver and glassware which make your contact lenses flash semaphore all evening. Striking sub-lieutenants in dashing uniforms stood to and wafted aft, and I kept thinking 'I must remember every detail of this' before I promptly forgot it. It's a disease I suffer from. It's called CRAFT, as in 'Can't Remember a F-----g Thing'. Would that Sara Kestelman had been there to describe it to you. The only bits I can accurately recall were the main course being pork, and that poor Poppet took to leaping around organizing an omelette, much to my embarrassment, when I would have been quite happy with a couple of potatoes and a mange tout or two. I also recall an incredible amount of drink being passed around and, after dinner, Poppet rising and mouthing to all the ladies 'Ladies, shall we withdraw and powder our noses?' I heard myself say, 'Not really? Really? Can't we stay, if we like, to bite the ends of their old cigars off?'

But we really *did* all pop upstairs, with Poppet, to the powder room and we – er, powdered. In the old days, of course, when the ladies withdrew, the fellas would point percy at the porcelain chamber pot in the sideboard, but I guess nowadays it's just cigars and whisky and Maxwell speculation. (Like *Questions:* Why can't you find Maxwell's grave in Israel? *Answer:* 'Cos it's in his wife's name.) I wouldn't begrudge them the cigars and the whisky, or even the percy pointing – but I'd be furious if I missed a good joke. Otherwise, it was a rivetingly good evening out and very jolly – tar.

Came the day of the dress rehearsal and after preview and with it came Julia McCarthy from her biopsy in London. Derek had given up his ground-floor dressing-room for her and we'd filled it with flowers. She was very pale and breathless but quite determined to be up to both shows, and do both shows she did. The boned bodices were hell against her biopsy scar and her voice was little more than a whisper. The effort of giving was so palpable that a less plucky mortal would have given up before the evening show. Pluck, however, was Julia's middle name and on she soldiered.

At the next day's rehearsal, the effort was etched

all over her face. During notes there was a fire alarm in the theatre and we all fled outside. By the time we returned, Braham, having come to the inevitable conclusion that Julia was not strong enough to carry on, had told her so as gently as he could. I don't know how relieved or how despairing she was. I only know that suddenly she was in a taxi and gone and that although I spoke to her fairly frequently in the next few weeks, I never saw her again. Within weeks she was in the St John and St Elizabeth Hospice and when Gwen and I tried to visit, we were told she had too many visitors and she was unable to get any rest. Dear lady, she is resting now and we all missed her amazing spirit.

Her part was eventually taken by Ann Way, that quaint and fine actress who has probably graced more films than Michael Caine in her time (and not a lot of people know that). With steely verve she seamlessly slotted into the dowager role. Malcolm Rennie, playing her son, coped very well with playing his scenes with three different mothers in as many weeks, but inevitably Julia's loss hovered over the production throughout its early incarnation and the balance of the comedy was in danger of tipping.

The first night came and went, as all first nights do, and the local reviews were good for us, for the play and, justifiably, for Paula: 'Understudy Paula Topham shines as Lady McPhail'. Of my performance, they said. 'The comedy proper starts when she arrives on stage'; for Derek, 'Plays his role with his customary gentle, bumbling humour'; and for the play, 'Pinero's comedy may have been written in 1890, but the pomposity and snobbery he punctures are familiar enough in genteel society today.' It was a review which reflected everything we'd all been striving towards.

That night we were given a celebratory drinks by the Friends of the Theatre Royal and then Derek dropped me off at my hotel and set off in search of his new lodgings, a stately country hotel, just over the border into Cornwall. He was more sober than most judges I've had the pleasure of meeting.

The next morning I met him outside the theatre. He was quite grey, haggard looking and, uncharacteristically, wearing the same clothes as the previous night. 'I've spent the evening in a police cell,' he told me, with a wry smile and an expression of mild crossness.

'Pardon?' I said, and over strong coffee he told me the events of the previous evening.

He'd been driving slowly, consulting the map as he searched for the route through the narrow roads, when a car had flashed its headlights close behind him, forcing him to stop. By the time the police, for it was they, got to his car they had already radioed Swansea and they knew exactly who he was. ''Ave you been celebrating then, Mr Nimmo?' they said. He was breathalized and taken to Plymouth police station, where he was thrown into clink, his regular medication taken away and his cufflinks removed. (This latter as a precaution against suicide. Now I know that there are many ways of attempting suicide, but death by cufflink?) He was then left, a man not in the first flush of youth, in October, in a cell, without a blanket, access to his beloved mobile phone, or food. Inclement treatment for a serial killer, but for a man who might or might not have been one over the eight after drinking a couple of glasses of M&S Chardonnay after a first night, I think erring on the side of over the top.

Apparently at midnight, a square in the cell door was opened a fraction and a man pushed through a cup of coffee. 'Mr Nimmo,' he said, 'Oi'd just like to thank you for all the hours of pleasure you've given me and moi family over the years.'

He was released on bail, having not slept a wink all night and told, interestingly, that had he been driving a *Lada* he would probably not have been stopped.

(Reminds me of a blackout sketch we used to do in revue:

Copper:	''Scuse me, sir, would you mind blowing into this?'
Man:	'But I haven't been drinking . . .'
Copper:	'Just do as I say, sir. Blow into this.'
Man:	'Oh, very well.' He blows. 'But I assure you . . .'
Copper:	'Thank you. And now, if you wouldn't mind blowing into this one.'
Man:	'But, officer, I haven't touched . . .'
Copper:	'Please sir, just do what I tell you and blow into this.'

Man: 'But – oh, all right.' He blows. 'But I
              promise you . . .'
Copper: 'Thank you very much, sir. Nothing I
              hate worse in the morning than putting
              on a pair of cold gloves.' Ba Boom.)

By the time he left the station at eight o'clock in
the morning, the press had been tipped-off, and by
the evening every paper in the south-west was
carrying a drunken driving rap on its front page.
Christmas was coming and they wanted an example
of too much Christmas spirits. They got one. And so
did we – one of the prices of fame.

We were due to open in London after the eight
week tour and, during those eight weeks we played
to standing room only, broke several box-office
records and, on the whole, had good press. Some
found the play fell between two shooting sticks, but
most described it as 'a comic delight to the eye' and
'a brilliant poke in the ribs of the English Upper
Classes', which, naïvely or not, is how I had always
seen it.

During the days we re-rehearsed, chopped,
changed, cut, put back and generally experimented,
during the evenings we tried it out on captive
audiences and during the nights we stomped comic-
ally round various hotel rooms with cramp and
indigestion.

On Sundays we fled by train, bus, Hondamatic
and hot air back to our loved ones to bank our
pittances, blink at our loved ones and launder our

smalls (getting smaller) for the next week away. In Guildford you couldn't get a seat if you pawned your mother-in-law's stockbroker. The play was accelerating in pace, the performances becoming surer, and on the whole our confidence was growing as the word of mouth grew more fulsome.

At Bath, I relaxed enough to shop. This is a good sign, though not necessarily for my accountant. (The boutique in question stocked clothes called Nipon and for some reason every single item on the rails leapt on to my body and refused to budge. I managed to stop at six outfits, telling myself they would be perfect for an upcoming *Jonathan Ross Show*. 'All SIX?' R.M., Accountant)

There are two ghosts in the Theatre Royal. A grey lady who drifts into Box A and a lucky butterfly which appears only when productions are going to be *very* successful. On the first night I lost my way back from the dressing-room to the hospitality drink upstairs and, fearful of the grey lady, went through the first door marked Exit. The door fell shut, leaving me outside, in the pouring rain locked in a gateless garden squared in by sharp railings. Upstairs, as people drank champagne and shrieked 'Darling you were average', the leading lady was damply banging on the windows shouting 'Let me in! Let me out!'. Lights came on in the windows around the square and people watched the floor-show bemusedly. Finally a bicycle-wheeling saviour gate-crashed the party, broke the news of my plight and I was humiliatingly rescued.

On the Thursday evening, in *October* remember, a beautiful winged creature in vivid red black and white fluttered into the conservatory set and perched on a banquette through Acts I and II. No, it wasn't Julian Clary, it was our lucky post-pupa, signalling success to a cast now quite light-headed with joy.

Then back home for Sunday's piles of old undies, a tentative 'Hi! – Bye!' to the kids and off again, this time to Newcastle. Now *there's* a city built to last. There the audiences didn't clap the sets, or the leading actors. They *listened*, made up their minds and finally rewarded us rapturously. There I walked on the freezing beach at Whitley Bay and learned how to breathe again. Somewhere along the tour I'd dropped a stone – and it wasn't in my shoe.

The publicity machine demanded interviews – London bums must be lured on to seats. In vain I tried to keep the subject on Pinero and off BT. My failure was on a grand scale: 'Lay off the BT stuff, Jonathan', I begged Mr Ross in the Hostility Room before the show, then froze behind the curtain as his entire introduction revolved round the phone. For twelve dizzy seconds I contemplated sodding off and leaving him to drench his Armani. On the thirteenth I went gloomily on and lacked lustre.

Final week. Brighton on Sea. Sara Kestelman and I shared a flat in the man-made Marina, and, like two kids at summer camp, we lived on puréed food, yoghurt and confessions and occasionally moped round the Asda superstore buying knickers. Our

director returned and we re-re-rehearsed, fine
tuned, prayed, yawned and rubbed Ralgex into the
bits the osteopath couldn't reach.

As we neared London, and headlines developed a
familiar 'ring'. I want you to envision the news press
montage you've so often seen in Hollywood movies,
Chicago Tribune! Dallas Monitor! LA Times!, only
here the headlines shout 'Beattie goes west', 'Beattie
to rescue', 'New lines for Beattie', 'Beattie's curtain
CALL' and 'Beattie rings the changes'. It put a
slight chill in the air but on we soldiered, foolishly
trying to talk about the play, rather than Alexander
Graham Bell's little folly.

The two London previews were nightmarish.
When you've played your last performance at
Brighton to a house filled to bursting point with
cheering punters, then opened in London to the
public equivalent of Death Valley, you wonder what
in hell's name happened between Sussex and Shaftesbury Avenue to cause such hostility. Braham was
the height of positiveness, in spite of having to sit out
there amongst it. 'You are all giving marvellously,'
he told us, 'and the show is in great shape – you
know London preview audiences, they haven't been
told what to think yet . . .' Poor lamb did his best and
better, but the chill descended further.

Opening night. London. The Albery Theatre. My
dressing-room looked like a Mafia funeral parlour
and smelled like Dolly Parton. Cards, telegrams and
last minute pep talks allayed the terror, only slightly.
(Jack and the kids poked tremulous noses round the

door at 6.30 and retreated knowing it was hallowed ground – no place for people whose stomachs lay in the usual place for stomachs.) There was wig glue in my ear and a toad in my throat.

At seven the curtain went up and at 9.30 it came down. The applause was genuine and the performances, said the director, couldn't have been bettered. Judderingly, fraily we ate our post theatre solids and unwound very slowly like hostages, getting re-accustomed to sunlight. Jack was very quiet.

Meanwhile, nine or ten assorted journalists tapped out their icy assessments into Dockland printing presses and returned, untroubled, to their Vodka Sours. A day's work done. And, even if you didn't read 'em, the message of doom gets through.

Then, all you have to do is go on. Because the show *must* go on. Or must it? (Answers please on a plain yellow envelope care of the Brazilian departure lounge, Heathrow. And Hurry!)

As for the Bath Butterfly . . . where *is* the little swine? Here boy! Here boy! Come and get your nice little drop of Formaldehyde . . . here boy!

So, I didn't read the reviews. Until now, six months later, and apart from one glorious rave from John Peters in the *Sunday Times*, they were as big a bunch of turkey droppings as ever left Wapping. The reason for Jack's gloom was more than just instinct. He had watched the critics during the interval. He had seen the critic of the *Jewish Chronicle*, David Nathan, hemmed in by fellow critics, all saying 'Why

are all these Jews involved in a play like this?' Their
renowned sensitivity had been somehow exacer-
bated by this fairly harmless piece of mild social
satire.

I still believe it's a play, very relevant to the
Eighties, about greedy people motivated entirely by
self-interest. Their loathing of Mr Lebanon, who
could indeed be of Lebanese or Persian extraction
equally well as he could be Jewish, derives from the
fact that they find him a vulgar upstart, not because
he is a Jew. Then, of course, the character has so
much charm and natural good humour that he
should emerge as the hero of the piece. It was
fantastical to me that it could be so misinterpreted.

What, I wondered, was the essential difference
between the production, by the same director, that
they'd seen and admired in Manchester and the one
which opened so painfully at the Albery? Well. Me.
I was a major difference. An actress whose religion
and creed was very well known was playing Lady
Kitty, who looks down on and out-manœuvres an
East End moneylender.

The following day the phone rang constantly with
newspapers wanting me to comment on Maureen
Paton's claims of anti-Semitism in the *Daily Express*.
Having not then read the comments, I said I thought
there was enough real prejudice in the world without
dreaming up new ones in 100-year-old plays. 'Beattie silenced by the critics' said the *Daily Express*.

I kept thinking of the late Graham Haberfield. He
was the stocky, raw young northern actor who

played Gerry Booth in *Coronation Street* for years. After he finally left, he took on the role of Winston in Jack's comedy series *The Dustbinmen*. One day when they were filming in Blackpool, Graham was growing more and more angry and disconsolate because of his treatment at the hands of the Gerry-fixated public.

'Hello, Gerry,' they'd call. ''Ow yer goin', Gerry?'

'Gorranother job yet, Gerry?' All the livelong day. It drove Graham, not uncharacteristically, to drink and he spent his evening getting remorselessly, blindly and intentionally drunk. On returning to his hotel, he staggered into the foyer where the police federation were winding up a function, and passed clean out in the lobby.

Graham awoke minutes later to find himself surrounded by policemen, all slapping his face and shaking him and all saying, to a man. 'All right now, Gerry? Come on, Gerry lad, you'll be all right now. On yer feet, Gerry, all right? How yer feeling, Gerry me old son?'

In our family, when someone rousingly calls out 'I thought *you'd* be driving a Rolls-Royce, Beattie, on what you must be earning', it's called 'doing a Gerry'.

Now here's the irony. After an initial pre-Christmas and post-reviews dip, we steadily built to some of the best houses in the West End, with standing room only Friday and Saturday. On word of mouth. The play was fun. Light, dazzling to look at and people seemed to find it *funny*. Once the initial gloom lifted we became a very contented, sociable and loving company. Helen Adie, who played two roles in the show, a stunning cameo of a French governess and a fractious Scots gel in Act III, had become romantically involved (sweet old-fashioned word for it) with our darkly charming stage manager, Simon Trewin, nephew of the late great JC, the critic. These things happen. As Tallulah Bankhead was wont to say 'on tour it doesn't count'. But they were both so appealing and very bright and it was lovely to see Helen tripping back and forth to the downstage right wings to while away the time between entrances by Simon's side as he worked the sound equipment.

Around Christmas time we had a 'grab bag'. This is where everyone in the company draws out a name from a hat and buys that person a gift, up to a certain amount. Then all the gifts are passed out and everyone gets to go 'oooh aaah, just what I wanted – what is it?' at the same time. After the ceremonials were over, Simon coughed and called the room together. We jeered and shouted in time-honoured fashion, expecting some kind of managerial moan about backstage noise and fag ends.

'Erm. I'd just like you all to know that . . . erm. Yesterday. I, erm, asked, er, Helen, to, erm, to be my wife and . . . erm . . . she said "yes".'

My dears, there wasn't a dry eye in the dressing-room. I was awash, of course. 'I feel like a Grandma', I wailed. It was just perfect and the immediate desire, of course, is to persuade *every* unmarried person in the vicinity to do the same hairbrained thing. Fortunately this passes. The wedding, I might tell you, was in June and as they Mendelssohn-marched through St Paul's Church, Covent Garden, you might have thought, by the amount I cried, that the whole thing was my doing and it was *my* daughter who was off to the Italian lakes on the morrow with confetti in her bra.

As for the rest of the run, it was all supper parties and birthday teas and hordes of titular folk in Lord Nimmo's suite and occasionally I'd bob in there of an evening and do my performing monkey act, not forgetting obeisance on the way out to John and his Roller. Derek's wife, Pat, is a saintly being who is one of God's great laughers and I shall treasure to my last wheeze the line-up of Sara, Gwen, Pat and myself faced with Princess Margaret and a couple of elegant vicars in the Nimmo suite, Sara bobbing sinuously, Gwen sweepingly, Pat Nimmo elegantly wafting carpetwards like the last act of *Camille*, and me jackknifing like someone who's just swallowed a conker but doesn't want to appear winded.

I didn't mention to Her Royal Highness what was perhaps my finest achievement to date. The restoration of the theatre loo. When we moved into the Albery Theatre after the previous tenants, *Blood Brothers*, had moved to the Phoenix, the downstairs lavatory had been a collectors' item. Peeling paint, hanging plaster, water running unchecked down the greasy walls, exposed dripping pipes and, somewhat scenically, a half-open roof through which pints of brown water dripped melodically into plastic buckets and thence to the unstructured lino floor, presumably providing a throbbing beat for Willy Russell's moody score. It had a certain outward bound charm but, it had to be said, I'd enjoyed my interact trips in there considerably more in the old Deborah Kerr days, when I'd last played the Albery. In those days Gryff, her company manager, usually had roses placed in the entrance and, dare one hint, a suggestion of wallpaper abutting the practical area.

I made a suggestion to the management that perhaps a lick of paint and some Blu-Tack might be an investment ... and they smiled and murmured words like 'We are ... any day now ... er ... it means digging up the forecourt of course ... er, temporary measures ...' and so on and so forth. Either the cast of *Blood Brothers* simply hadn't noticed how wet they were each night or the management had told them a shaggy bog story rather like the one they'd just told me. In my book, however, sanitary arrangements are necessary to sanity arrangements, and I continued my harangue up to and including the first night party where I hijacked the management and talked loudly and lavatorially across the heads of the captains of industry and show business. The next day the workmen arrived and sealed up the streaming, running, dripping walls, patched up the floor and added, thoughtfully, a ceiling. I would venture to say my cup runneth

over. Thank you notes were posted off and it was
with a merry spring in my step that I ventured into
work the following evening.

As I entered my dressing-room the smell of drains
almost blew me back upstairs. Obviously something
noxious had been diverted. I could live with it, or I
could start another campaign. Sigh. Or I could
change in the new green loo. I headed for it, stopped
in my tracks and peered in front of me. High on the
door was shiny new brass plate engraved with the
words 'The Maureen Lipman Memorial Loo' with
date, year and scale of endeavour beneath. Alone, in
the depths of the theatre, like some demented
Phantom I bellowed with laughter until it was
almost too late for me to make it to what was so
elegantly mahoganized within. Nimmo. Need I say
more?

One day, between matinée and evening, I threw a
children's party for the cast. My dresser Sally and I
decorated our pungent quarters with balloons and
streamers, spread a large paper cloth on the floor,
paper hats, blowers, party favours and things throw-
able. We had piles of sandwiches, half white, half
brown – I got quite tearful whilst slicing off the
crusts. How many years ago was it since those
obligatory, wondrous, enervating (whichever way
round that means) days? Days of praying for sun-
shine, of icing Batman's webbing and Joan Collins'
eyelashes 'til two in the morning, of wrapping layer
after layer, toffee between each layer, present au
milieu, 'Nellie the Elephant' set ready in the tape

recorder, celery and cream cheese, Dolly Mixtures, lemon curd and Marmite and blessed, blessed 'Dead Lions' to take the lunatic glint out of their eyes before their mothers arrived? Heigh ho. Nowadays it's 'Is i' alrigh 'f sumo the lads come over?' followed by a massive pizza delivery, snooker, moonlight football, huge sleeping-bagged forms all over the floors, total decimation of the cornflake supplies and no milk save the pools on the floor.

So there I was, (before I so whimsically interrupted myself) at home a-butterin' and a-spreadin' and a-pourin' jelly into fluted paper dishes with nary a thought of transportation. Once in the theatre, Sally forged ahead whilst I got through the histrionics of Act III as speedily as possible, filling bowls with Hula Hoops and Twiglets and laying out the iced buns and baby sausages in pretty patterns.

At first, like all the best three year olds, the cast was a little shy and I felt very Joyce Grenfell as I ushered them into their places on the carpet. But, before you could say 'George, don't do that', they were throwing food at one another and we were off. With fourteen entertainers as guests, who needs Smarty Arty? You should have seen the way those actors knocked back the honey sandwiches – you'd think they'd been 'resting' since *Z Cars*. We passed the parcel and had tantrums when we didn't win and confessed to Ribena withdrawal symptoms, and I like to think that some of us were sick on each other, too. Then lots of 'Thank you for having me''s and back into whalebone and britches for the evening show.

Towards the end of the run, I put in an early-morning TV appearance in aid of 'Tommy's Campaign' at St Thomas's Hospital. It's a charity formed to raise money for better prenatal care and I romped around outside St Thomas's wearing, I seem to recall, a black-and-white bouclé suit and a blue spotted potty on my head. Let's face it, they come no cheaper than me, turn-wise. That evening, I parked in Garrick Street and, cutting through the alley on my way to the theatre, I was stopped, as usual, by two resident vagrants on the scrounge for a 'cuppa tea, Maureen, thanks love'. I gave them 50p and strode on. After the show, I encountered the same pair who said 'Saw you this morning on TV Maureen – very good cause that, what was it?' I told them. 'Yeah – very worthwhile Maureen.'

'You've got a TV then?,' I couldn't help but enquire.

'Oh yeah, Maureen. All mod cons – nice flat they've give us. Council. TV, everything ...' and before I could burble anything further, he added, 'Tell you what, Maureen – take this for all the little babies. Go on, take it, no, go on.' He thrust 50p into my hands – no doubt mine – and said, 'Keep up the good work, gel.' For a moment I felt curiously like Crocodile Dundee.

The show ended its run with full houses and a close company worried only about where its next job was coming from. For me, *je ne regrette rien*. It was, in retrospect, that most honourable of things: a good job well done, with some good friends – medium rare – and some glamorous photos – very rare indeed – for my front room cabinet.

Cinema Scope

In 1968 I played my first major film role in Peter Collinson's *Up the Junction*. At the time, I saw my future as a couple of films a year punctuated by the odd hit play. In fairness, my arrogance wasn't exclusive. We all thought it was our birthright, being as the British film industry was booming. Blooming even. Rooted in Ealing, watered by wartime, fed by kitchen sink and given a veritable flower show by the Swinging Sixties. The rest was a silent movie – until the Chariot rolled off the tracks, paving the way for our actors to clutch Oscars and our producers to clutch straws. Pinewood is desolate – an empty film set of a film set where commercials are made by out-of-work film directors. The restaurant in the panelled dining room is resoundingly unpeopled, the topiaried lawns devoid of ghosts let alone people. It's like a lovable Old English sheepdog wagging its tail in Battersea Dogs' Home in the hope of finding a good home, whilst all the adults walk past looking for Lassie.

France reveres its film-makers and the French turn out in droves for indigenous films. Here in England, land of *Kind Hearts and Coronets*, *The Elephant Man*, *Oliver*, *Brief Encounter* et al, nothing has changed since the war – we're still queuing up for Yankee imports. Handsome, charming imports flawed by chronic sentimentality (see *City Slickers* and the snappily titled *Fried Green Tomatoes at the Whistle Stop Café*; or rather see some of them and close your eyes and make ambulance noises during the homespun philUSsophy.)

Back home, the few films made have a new and puzzling flaw: why are the secondary character parts, at which we used to bestride the globe, so grossly over-played in modern British movies? Have we had to relinquish our fine character work in order to win leading man status? I thought the first half hour of *Hear My Song* was painfully overdone – fortunately I rarely leave a film half-way through, but the balls of my feet were raring to go. I'm glad they didn't. Once Ned Beatty, on whom the picture was, I presume, financed, had clocked into work, the picture achieved its objective. We cared about someone and were enchanted again.

Before I'm denounced as a prime participant in this 'Mug for the Movies' trend, I should own up. My last role was that of Esmeralda, a mean Spanish noblewoman, in the brand new, long awaited (as in twenty-three years) Carry On film, *Carry on Columbus*.

Now this for me was an exciting proposition: a) it was a film; b) it was a film with a part for *me* in it; c) it would probably be made *and* released; and d) I could probably do my seven days' filming and, amongst all those old and new stars of TV and, er, TV, not even be noticed doing it. One of those suppositions was wrong. Kindly circle the appropriate misconception and you could win a night out with the Grumbleweeds at any Romanian Theme Park of Your Choice. I've never seen so much publicity for an unreleased film. It was as if Cher, Jodie Foster, Sean Connery and Julia Roberts had all been fired on the first day to make way for Jim Dale, Bernard Cribbins and Julian Clary. I even made *Hello!* magazine. Wearing a tall black hat, plaited earphones and black-and-gold embroidered robes, and looking like a cross between the late Archbishop Makarios and Yentl the Shivabocha, I thought wistfully of the black-and-gold Olivier Awards dress (now known as the 'Eat your heart out, Kathleen, gown'), which never even made the 'Where are they now?' section of *Pig Farmers' Weekly*, and a small high pitched sound escaped my lips.

When I first read the script I assumed I would be playing Esmerelda as a Spaniard. With her first appearance being as a part of the King of Spain's court and her first line being, 'My husband, the Count, has got the Canaries.' (TWO nights out with the Grumbleweeds in any Isle of Wight disco of your choice if you can guess the reply – thank you, that's the lady in the second row with the pudding-basin haircut and the banana up her blouse). 'Is he in much pain?' – I didn't think that was too much of a wild guess. I rather liked the idea of essaying 'dath a bery nithe voat wheech chew are thailing Mithter Columvus.' One phone call dashed my hopes.

'No,' said the producers. 'If you play it Spanish, then everyone will have to play it Spanish.' This is not the Carry On Way of carrying on. I stared at the part for a few days hoping for inspiration and finally had a chat with the author, the amicable Dave Freeman.

'Dave, er – I'm not sure I've quite got the handle on Esmeralda yet . . . er, the character, I mean, er, I just wondered whether you see her as pretentious nouveau riche, or very upper crust or . . .'

'Well, she's determined to marry off her daughter to this rich old man,' he told me helpfully, 'and she's got this wedding to . . .'

'Yes, I realize that's the story and I know she's pretty mercenary, it's just I'm not entirely sure of what to do with her – I mean the lines in themselves are not . . . well, they *are funny*, but I usually have a physical grasp of . . . you know, it's just turning up on day one without a rehearsal and . . .'

'Yes, yes, I do see your problem,' he mused. Then, 'Tell you what, love, have you thought of having a fan?'

I got my motivation. In one. Turn up. Know your

lines. Don't bend them. Then go for it.

The first day of filming, a polite early morning call at the studio, I stand in three layers of black wool and meet my daughter, Holly Aird, her maidservant, Rebecca Lacey in the Barbara Windsor neckline, Su Douglas and Jon Pertwee, who's got his vocal tic all ready and worked out. I have decided to go for the *facial* tic, an upper lip twitch reminiscent of my last close encounter with the cat litter. Just in case it's a total failure, I'm carrying a fan.

The director, Gerald Thomas, is a gentle man, in the true sense of both words. Kindly, avuncular and charming, he is a veteran of thirty-one *Carry Ons*, and is still amusing and amused by the whole charabanc. His first words after I delivered my first tremulous lines were, 'Thank you. Very nice. Next scene.' Well you could have knocked me sideways with Julian Clary's comb! Accustomed as I am to the BT shoots where. 'Hello? Is that you, Dolly?' could last, and often *did* last, an afternoon, I was utterly discombobulated.

Of course, this was a picture whose budget is probably one-quarter of Marlon Brando's auto-prompt operator's salary and, therefore, there was no instant playback monitor. Which saves an enormous amount of re-takes. Obviously if a crowd of producers gather round take forty then there are likely to be six or seven opinions on whether or not there should be a take forty-one. If you are just relying on the wisdom, experience and taste of the director and he's in as big a hurry to get on as the producers, then 'Thank you. Very nice. Next scene. Carry on', makes a lot of sense.

Filmically the *mix* is the danger. In the right-hand corner you've got yer diehards and yer stalwarts led by the ever youthful Jim Dale, late of *Six Five Special*, *Carry on Cowboy*, *Barnum* and Broadway. He lives in New York with his second wife, Julie, who runs a prestigious art gallery in an Art Nouveau filled apartment on Fifth Avenue, and a hundred and eighty acres of upstate New York with his own lakes. In the plural. Yet he jumped at the chance to Carry On Carrying On, in the company of past revellers Bernard Cribbins, Jack Douglas, Jon Pertwee, Leslie Phillips and June Whitfield. There were several rumours buzzing around as to the reason for the marked absence of Barbara Windsor, Bernard Bresslaw and Kenneth Connor – but the sensible if not the most gossip-worthy one is that they were doing a *Carry On* summer season at Blackpool. There were lots of stories of the good old days, which when you come down to it were probably not that great since I'm told the entire cast were on set every day whether they were needed or not, and the most the inimitable Kenneth Williams ever received was £3,000. Professional to the red dots in the corners of their eyes, they will discuss visual gags and physical 'business' in the tones that David Attenborough and Desmond Morris might discuss the mating techniques of the Kakapo Parrot, and for me, the avowed people watcher, it was fascinating.

Jim reminisced about a long and wisely forgotten

Restoration play in which we'd once appeared at the Old Vic. It was an undiscovered Goldsmith called *The Good Nature'd Man*. I might add it has remained so ever since. His character was an uppity society climber who was after the hand of the bookish and introverted heiress, Miss Richland. Me! Bookish and introverted! You see – no such thing as type casting when you're twenty-three, green as mushy peas and nobody's heard of you.

Any road up (and aren't they all these days, particularly in the wet weather at rush hour?), for his first entrance Jimbo had worked out a gag involving a flying cloak. He walked in with a bow and a flourish and proceeded to walk up his own cloak in such a way that the tie around his throat began to strangle him as he tripped over and the whole cloak flew backwards over his head and settled in slow motion over his pone body like a shroud. As Jim tells it, the director, John Dexter, was so thrilled with the business, being a huge music-hall comic fan himself, that he sent a message to the head of our company, Sir Laurence Olivier, to come to the rehearsal room to see it. Which he did. Afterwards the great man congratulated Jim but said, and here we need Anthony Hopkins to do the perfect impersonation, 'Jim, dear, clever old chap that you are, it's simply marvellous, but you know you can't do it. It's too dangerous. Far, far too dangerous and we value you too much to let you risk it night after night.'

After he left, John Dexter, not known for thinking the best of his fellow man, said 'It was too good. The old sod's going to use it for himself. You wait.' To my knowledge he never did, but the gag went and in its place came the hat gag where, on introduction, Jim took off his hat revealing a wig which had been set with a vat of talcum powder. In mid doff the entire cast was concealed by a fine cloud of dust and all you could hear were bronchial barks. It *was* funny. All the rest of us had to do was follow it with undiscovered Goldsmith.

Meanwhile, in the far left-hand corner were what are often referred to as the Alternative Comedians. Whence comes this appellation? Alternative Comedy must be like alternative medicine, favoured by those who are fed up with the traditional approach, frowned upon by the old practitioners and dabbled in by most people on the grounds it can't harm, without ever throwing away the Paracetamols. Is Alternative Comedy holistic? Is it a new treatment for the body politic? Of course not. It's just new faces. New talent. New angle. No modern stand-up will ever be more shocking or more dangerous than Lenny Bruce. The trick is nowadays to avoid slick or ingratiating behaviour. Never ask your audience for approbation. Ignore them. In spite of Clive Anderson's ready wit, *Whose Line is it Anyway?* is often as embarrassing as our first year improvisation class at RADA. In those days the fun sport was to get on a tube train in a separate compartment from your fellow student, then at the following station make a dramatic entrance into his compartment, walk through the length of the car, slap him resoundingly

across the face and yell 'Do you *know* you are the
father of my unborn child?' At nineteen we found
this an incredible scream, why should I assume that
nineteen-year-olds today would find it other than
likewise? Friday night's *Rory Bremner Show* followed
by *Have I Got News for You?* are the only shows I
would stay in for. Bremner because, at last, an
impersonator's scripts are every bit as good as his
voices. And oh, the wisdom of placing the two Johns,
Bird and Fortune and those alarming armchairs for
'In Conversation'. Fortune's face has refused to
settle into middle-age and as a consequence the
small boy is fighting the middle-aged man, every
inch of the way, and will continue to do so until he
looks completely deranged. Rather like Patrick
Moore. Together with John Bird, the maniacal pixie
concealed beneath the civil servant, they make
alternatives mainstream.

Since none of the people I've mentioned over the
last 350 words are in *Carry on Columbus*, you could
be forgiven for wondering whether I've just lost the
gist of my quest for jest (try saying that after a
Carling Black Label). So who did we have? Well
there was Rik Mayall and Nigel Planer who I only
encountered at the initial get-together, where Gerald Thomas and my mother discovered they were
practically from the same street. Mayall is, I don't
know if you know, ridiculously handsome. He once
spoke to me at the gym. I didn't realize who he was
because his mobile features hide his good looks from
the TV viewer (this is a diplomatic way of saying he

pulls faces on the telly) and I almost fell over the plié machine. I did encounter Alexei Sayle, whom I first saw in the early Eighties doing a simply terrifying monologue about a Ford Cortina, at the Comedy Store. Either time has mellowed him or he saves his anger for the front stalls, because he seemed to be a rather benign, friendly sort of chap, if somewhat bemused by what he was doing there, saying the lines as written. Julian Clary is a real beauty and rather shy. Rather normal actually. The sort of boy your mother would be pleased if you brought home. At first. He fractured his foot during the filming. 'I wasn't doing *anything*. I just sort of walked on it and I heard this snap . . .' so there was a frailty about him which added to the charm.

There is of course a tradition of camp humour in the Carry Ons. In England. In fact, when my friend Astrid came to live in this country from the States, she actually thought that most of British entertainment involved men dressed in women's clothing. Danny La Rue was in his heyday, Benny Hill and Dick Emery favoured the same handbags, Stanley Baxter ran amok each Hogmanay and Carry On films were peppered with hairy legs in stilettos. Also, her new husband had just written the music for the stage musical *Privates on Parade*, starring Dennis Quilley in Carmen Miranda turbans and strategically placed bananas. Amazingly enough, she's still in England.

The Comic Strip was represented by Peter Richardson and Keith Allen who were not entirely happy with the fairly rigid format. Keith is a comic with an air of barely suppressed danger about him and a tendency to rip off his clothing at the least possible provocation. Then somewhere in the middle are the American actors Charles Fleischer, voice of Roger Rabbit, and Larry Miller, and the English actors Richard Wilson (who, in the days when Pinewood was a production village and every inhabitant was in the movies, would have played all the Richard Wattis parts), Sara Crowe, Alan Carduner and, I suppose, me, doing the Hattie Jacques role – flyweight version. Heigh Ho! All will have been revealed by the time you read this and I'll either be queuing up to appear in *Carry on Fergie* or hiding from Barry Norman somewhere with a Tesco's carrier bag over my head.

The actual shooting was quiet, orderly and sedate, beginning promptly at 8.00 am and never finishing later than six. The budget was so tight that for the first time ever, in *my* experience, we paid for our own breakfast, lunch and tea. Still, the atmosphere was a happy one and the set was always open to children, pets, old people and various crews filming the crews filming the crews filming the filming. *Fitzcarraldo* with codpieces.

One day, on the deck of Columbus's ship, I was surprised to see nine small bespectacled Indian nuns in grey and white habits. 'What scene do the nuns come in?' I asked Maggie the marvellously contained continuity lady, who was a veteran of almost every David Lean film ever made, and must have a book in her bursting to be written.

'No. They're *real* nuns,' she replied. 'They run a small hotel nearby where the lighting cameraman is staying – so he asked them on the set.'

Standing chatting to them in full black and gold costume, wearing heavy foundation cream, lip-gloss and bag eraser, I marvelled at the unlined beauty of their skins. The Mother Superior, in her last year before being called to Rome, looked about fifteen. All that giggling must help of course, apart from the clear consciences.

On another day, the entire England football squad turned up. Twenty-six toned, clear-eyed, tightly-muscled young men and their managers Graham Taylor and Laurie McMenemy. It was almost too much for the female contingent and several attacks of the vapours came on. Probably from the laced corsets, we told ourselves mendaciously.

I, apparently, behaved in my best Joyce Grenfell manner. I didn't really know I was doing it but apparently I swanned down the staircase saying, 'Hello! *Hello!* and you must be John Barnes – *gosh* my son would be happy to be here today. And where might Rob Jones be? Oh, *there* you are! *Hello* – it's Gary Lineker isn't it? Now how is George doing? Really? Oh that's wonderful.' I then stood at the foot of the steps after they'd all been shown round the set, grasping each player by the hand and saying 'Good to meet you and good luck with Brazil', like an uninvited, untutored version of the Duke of Edinburgh. Bluff your way at sportsmanship. Holly and Rebecca were helpless with laughter.

On the last day of shooting we had a 'wrap' party in the Pinewood Green Room. It was a balmy night and the relief flowed out with the food and wine. Producer John Goldstone had heard tales of my recent surprise outing to see 'The Chippendales'. I'd regaled the make-up girls and secretaries with hair-raising stories of monstrous regiments of women screaming for action. Consequently, he'd hired their English equivalents, 'The Dreamboats' to do the cabaret. Boy, did they have the wrong audience. No sooner had the boys started to peel off their 'Officer and a Gentleman' togs than every heterosexual man in the room disappeared in search of fresh salmon and fresh air, leaving about twenty-odd girls sitting on the floor trying desperately to sound like a thousand women screaming for sex. Including me, whose fault the entire thing seemed to be. My penance was to have my face ground relentlessly into the crutch of a greasepainted grinder and to appear to like it. As the gyrating and miming escalated, Keith Allen appeared bearing a tray of drinks and calling 'Your drinks, Miss Lipman'. It goes without saying that he was stark naked. It was a surprise. Not a big one, but a surprise. It was a good evening. I'd worked for only seven days, but I said goodbye to a family.

Why do I love filming so much? Partly for that family feeling. Partly because of the waiting around for hours just to sparkle for seconds. I really *love* not working, when I've got a job. Forgive me for this appalling confession, particularly when so many people are desperate to work. After three weeks without a job, I'm as wavery as a pie-frill. Migraine, low back pain, palpitations, creeping senility, you name it, I'll bore for Europe on it. But give me a slow day on a film set, when the second unit camera car's gone missing in Esher, the lighting operator's down with Lyme's disease and the producers are strangling each other in a Winnebago, then you can be certain there's one gleeful woman on the set.

Future to the Back

So. Onwards. After three months completing the book I wasn't going to write, I'm about to go back to work. It's a play by Neil Simon called *Lost in Yonkers*. I play the part of Bella, the somewhat retarded daughter of a tyrannical German–American matriarch. It's a Pulitzer Prize-winning play which tears at your heartstrings and patches up the tears with tears of laughter. English critics are renowned for their snobbishness towards American plays in general and Neil Simon in particular, I think because he commits the heinous crime of making it look easy. So far I've had one Brooklyn accent lesson with Joan Washington and tomorrow I'm taking a trip to a home for the mentally handicapped to meet some people who have Bella's problem. In my heart I know I'm made for this role and in my stomach and other low down bits I'm convinced I will fail. The evergreen Rosemary Harris is cast as my mother and we open in town in November. I'm a woman on the verge of nervous shakedown.

On Sunday I do a presentation for Air France then race to the airport for our annual 'too weak' holiday in Majorca. When I return I do two shows of *Re:Joyce*, one at Southwold to raise money for Denbigh Hall and one at Chichester to raise some for me and Den. The following day I start a drama documentary about Enid Blyton, who was almost nothing like she seemed. Three days later I start *Lost in Yonkers*. Four weeks' rehearsal, seven weeks' touring, six months, please God, playing in the West End. Which theatre? I don't know yet. But recently I went to see *Heartbreak House* at the Haymarket Theatre and the barman said how much he was looking forward to my play coming in there. Am I arguing? If anyone knows what's going on in this business, in this town, it's a good barman.

Oh, and on Thursday, I'm meeting Loekie, the Dutch iridologist and kinesiologist (another 'olo-gist?) She's going to help me find out what causes my-graines. On Thursday Paul the cranial osteopath will call round. The only thing I haven't tried is execution, and I may wait till the second night of *Yonkers* for that.

Meanwhile, I'm not to worry what Amy's going to do in her year off. It's not my business. She's told me that. Also it's too early to decide. Or which University she will choose. Bite my overbite and shut up. And I'm to be *very* patient and very pleasant to my mother in Majorca – because who knows how many holidays we'll be able to spend together in the future, and no biting remarks about Adam's sartorial disarray or Jack's smoking or whether Esperanza will be bringing the baby to work with her after she's had it, and I'm not to take out a contract on David Irving's life, or head butt the boys who stole Adam's new bike outside Cherry Tree Woods, when I find them, and I *will* choose the wallpaper for the conjugal bedroom so that we can take down the twenty-five assorted scraps that have given that familiar crazy-paving look, erstwhile unseen since the days of D-I-Y covered wastepaper baskets. Also I will return some of those dinner party invites ... Tom and Kara, Geoff and Marilyn, Johnny and Andrea, Bernard and Judith, Lila, Claire, Ivor and Judy, George and Penny, Jeremy and Carole, are you there? Can you hear me? I've got an American cookbook now which measures in cups and spoons only, and I've changed the dining room into the living room and vice versa ... it's only taken me eleven years to realize that the door from the front room leading through the utility room to the kitchen is there because the front room is a dining room not a lounge and *that's* why I could never get the bloody seating right!

When I set out to write this book, its projected title was *Even the Freesias Smelled of Fish*. It came to me one day as I lay in the Portland Hospital basking, fermenting even, in mega self-pity. 'Can you bring me my cream nightie, Jack, and my dressing-gown, the red one. Oh, and my non-allergic orthopaedic pillow? The one on my side of the bed?' It only hit me after their arrival, with a small bunch of my favourite flowers, that they all were permeated with the same smell. The smell of my house. And what exquisite fragrance was that? Fried fish, that's what. Appalling realization. I have one of *those* houses. The ones I recall visiting as a child with my parents. Each one had its own distinctive smell. My grand-mother's: boiled chicken downstairs and mothballs up. My great-aunt: cat pee. Everywhere. My par-ents' friends: monkey nuts. My best friends' houses: mostly baking and washing. A schoolfriend's: cab-bage and ironing. Our house, after a long trip to one of their houses: er, fish. Not unpleasant fishy, dockside fish. Not chip shop, sweet oniony fish. Just fish. Fried into the wallpaper and the lino, and the chaircovers. In spite of the spraying and the fanning and the window and door opening. There it was. As I said earlier, you can take the girl out of Hull ...

'And why,' I can hear the girl's companion of twenty-three years saying, 'would you want to? Best olfactory sensation in the world. Knocks spots off "Amarige" and I know what *that* costs 'cos I took out a second mortgage to get it for your last birthday.' Of course, we don't smell the smell ourselves unless we're returning from two weeks in alien surround-ings. Then, like the man says, it's a fragrance that's too rare and too precious to bottle.

So I changed the title to *Not Known in These Parts*. The cover would feature the writer in vamp dress, fishnet tights, scarlet lips and nails, veiled hat and seven inch tart's shoes, clinging brazenly to a large, hairy, well-muscled, preferably male, leg. Just the one. All I had to do was locate an amenable leg. Shouldn't be too difficult round this neck of the woods . . . 'Er, hello, is that the Strand Theatre, backstage? Er, Maureen Lipman speaking. I wonder if, by any chance, it's possible to rent out the leg of a Chippendale – just by the hour? No, I realize I'd have to take the upholstered parts as well . . .' Or: 'Hello Mr Taylor, Graham, how *are* you? Fine. Good. Yes. Sorry about the European champion-ships, I was wondering, erm, any of your boys laid up with an injury at present? You know, something minor, tendon strain or what have you . . . er . . . just in the one leg, wants to earn a bob or two . . .?' Or: 'Hello, Hellooooo, Mrs Schwarzenegger . . . can your Arnold come out to play?' The possibilities are endless. I mentioned the idea to my mother on the phone the other night.

'How do you mean "just a leg"?' she said. 'What's that got to do with being *Not Known in These Parts*? What parts?' I opened my mouth to reply and she added, 'Anyway. *When's it coming out?*'